ANTHROPOLOGICAL PAPERS

MUSEUM OF ANTHROPOLOGY, UNIVERSITY OF MICHIGAN

No. 7

The Crable Site, Fulton County, Illinois

A Late Prehistoric Site in the Central Illinois Valley

by

HALE GILLIAM SMITH

ANN ARBOR
UNIVERSITY OF MICHIGAN PRESS, 1951

ISBN (print): 978-1-949098-36-5
ISBN (ebook): 978-1-951519-60-5

Browse all of our books at
sites.lsa.umich.edu/archaeology-books.

Order our books from the University of Michigan
Press at www.press.umich.edu.

For permissions, questions, or manuscript queries,
contact Museum publications by email at umma-pubs@umich.edu or visit the Museum website at
lsa.umich.edu/ummaa.

CONTENTS

ILLUSTRATIONS

THE CRABLE SITE
FULTON COUNTY, ILLINOIS

INTRODUCTION

The only scientific work done at the Crable site (known also as the Bluff City site and the Crabo site) was that of the University of Chicago Expedition in 1933 and a prior excavation by the University of Illinois.[1] The University of Chicago Expedition did not work the site in its entirety, an undertaking which time and the condition of the area did not allow; therefore, key points throughout the area were selected for intensive study. For a number of years before 1933, however, the site had been a digging ground for local amateur archaeologists. The McGirr Collection, now in the Dickson Mound State Park Collection, has 165 pottery vessels from this site. The park is located southeast of Lewiston, Illinois.

This paper presents both the results of work done by the University of Chicago and the information secured by local collectors so that a very complete presentation is given of the affiliations of Crable in late prehistoric or protohistoric times. (Protohistoric is used here in the sense in which it was used by Strong in his work on the northern Great Plains.)[2]

The Crable site at one time was believed to belong to the Spoon River Focus, but the cultural material has certain definite features setting it off from other Middle Mississippi sites of the region. Other excavated Middle Mississippi sites in the area are the Rose Mound Group,[3] the Dickson Mound,[4] Kingston Lake,[5] Crabtree,[6] and the University of Chicago excavations of $F^{V}664$, $F^{O}34$, $F^{O}12$, $F^{O}13$, $F^{O}14$, $F^{V}35$, and $F^{V}49$.[7]

[1] There is some material at the University of Illinois under the name of Crabo, which was procured by A. R. Kelly before the University of Chicago excavation.

[2] Strong, 1940, p. 377.

[3] Griffin and Morgan, editors, 1941, p. 22.

[4] Cole and Deuel, 1937, p. 120.

[5] Simpson, 1936, pp. 50-52.

[6] Snyder, 1908, pp. 33-43.

[7] Cole and Deuel, *op. cit.*

ACKNOWLEDGMENT

I wish to thank the Department of Anthropology of the Universit of Chicago for the privilege of using the field notes, laboratory facilities, and cultural material from the Crable site and for permission to publish this report. I am indebted also to Dr. Fay-Cooper Cole for his instruction and co-operation, to Dr. Donald Dickson for permission to study the McGirr Collection and other data, and to Mr. Donald Wray for the use of his unpublished work on the Kingston Lake site. Thanks are due also Dr. James B. Griffin, Director of the Museum of Anthropology, of the University of Michigan, for his suggestions and co-operation, and for permission to use the negatives of the Oneot jars from the Crable site in the Dickson Mound State Park Collection.

THE LOCATION, DESCRIPTION, AND GEOLOGY OF CRABLE

The Crable site was excavated by the Department of Anthropology of the University of Chicago during the field season of 193 the last of a series of five summers' work in Fulton County. The field party was under the direction of Thorne Deuel. Assistants were Georg Neumann, osteologist; J. D. Jennings, supervisor of excavation; Paul Cooper, photographer; and Robe Braidwood, surveyor and draftsman.

The Crable site was opened by the same methods and techniques that were used by the University of Chicago in all their excavations in Fulton County. For a detailed account of these methods, see Cole and Deuel in Rediscovering Illinois.[8]

The Crable site is in the extreme southeast part of Fulton County, the southwest corner of Section 31, Kerton Township (latitude: 40° 11' 19" N.; longitude: 90° 12' 48" W.). The sit is on the summit of the west bluff paralleling the Illinois River and is owned by Mr. Norman Crable. The nearest town of any size is Havana, county seat of Mason County, ten miles northeast of Crable.

[8] *Ibid.*, pp. 22-32.

In this section of the country the bluffs rise 125 to 175 feet above the bottoms or flood plains of the river valley. They are usually rather steep, in some places rising in elevation 100 feet or more in a horizontal distance of approximately 300 feet (see Map 1). Above the abrupt escarpment the plateau or tableland is rounded back from the brink of the bluffs until a plain is formed a few hundred feet from the edge of the drop. The terrain toward the interior tends to be slightly rolling, lacking the emphatic contours of the bluff region.

A bird's eye view of the 600-foot contour of the bluffs (the contour line above the steep section of the bluff) shows an uneven line indented by deeply eroded gullies and washes, following a course generally parallel to the river. The eroded washes have given the steep peripheral parts of the bluffs a ragged profile. In general, the contours of the brink conform to those of the basal contours at the foot of the bluff. Since erosion has affected the summit plateaus very little, their horizontal profile is uniformly level unless interrupted by artificial changes in topographical features, such as roads.

The Crable site covers the highest part of the bluff plateau for considerable distance and includes several spurs which project out past the main line of the bluff. Over the 10-acre area occur an extensive village site (Fv891), a cemetery (Fc896), conical mounds (Fo892, Fo893, Fo894, Fo895), a pyramidal mound (Fo898), and a large fire pit (Fm897). On the spur of the bluff to the southeast of Fo898 are large aboriginal cemeteries (not shown on the map).

The village site, where the terrain permitted, had been under cultivation for a number of years prior to excavation. The uncultivated parts of the region, which were wooded, had been given over to pasture land. The soil geology is uniform over the entire summit of the bluff region. Near the edge of the bluff and on the ends of spurs are deep deposits of loess or wind-laid yellow or grayish yellow deposits. A thin layer of forest humus overlies the loess deposit. This humus did not prove to be of uniform thickness throughout the area of excavations.

The ground water, containing carbonic acid, has leached out the calcium of the loess down to an average depth of 2 to 3 feet. Below this zone, where the calcium reaction is not observed, concretions (secondary deposition of calcium) are found. After a 2-foot zone of concretions the loess becomes a darker gray with a strong calcium content. In retreating toward the interior, a few feet from the edge of the bluff to the more level area, the soil profile changes to some extent. The gray forest humus, 6 to 8 inches thick, overlies a 2-foot stratum of weathered loess which is red-brown and has no calcium content. This weathered loess gently grades into unweathered loess of the yellow observed at points near the edges of the bluff. This zone has a strong calcium content within 8 inches of its upper limits. The lack of weathered loess on the spurs and edges of the bluff is due to constant erosion caused by speedier drainage of rain at these points.[9]

EXCAVATIONS

The Village Site, Fv891

The village site covers approximately ten acres northwest of the mound group and follows the rounded edge of the ridge. Over the surface of the entire area are found sherds, flint chips, broken human and animal bones, charcoal, pieces of polished stone, and red ochre. Approximately in the center of the village site is a large truncated mound, Fo898, which at present, after years of cultivation, is 15 feet high.[10]

The cultural surface material is found only on the highest part of the bluff, some distance back from the abrupt "break" of the sides of the escarpment. The axis of this highest area is in a general southwestern and northeastern direction. Most of the sherds and other cultural material from the village site were obtained from surface collections and not by excavations. Considerable material was noted over the entire area of the village, but it was somewhat more plentiful near the southern edge of the western end, at a point where the decline toward the edge of the bluff was pronounced. Two test pits were excavated in this section at points south and west of mound Fo898 (indicated on Map 1 as A and B).

[9] Root, 1938.

[10] In a personal communication Donald Wray reported that ash layers were found in the mound, showing periods of destruction and rebuilding.

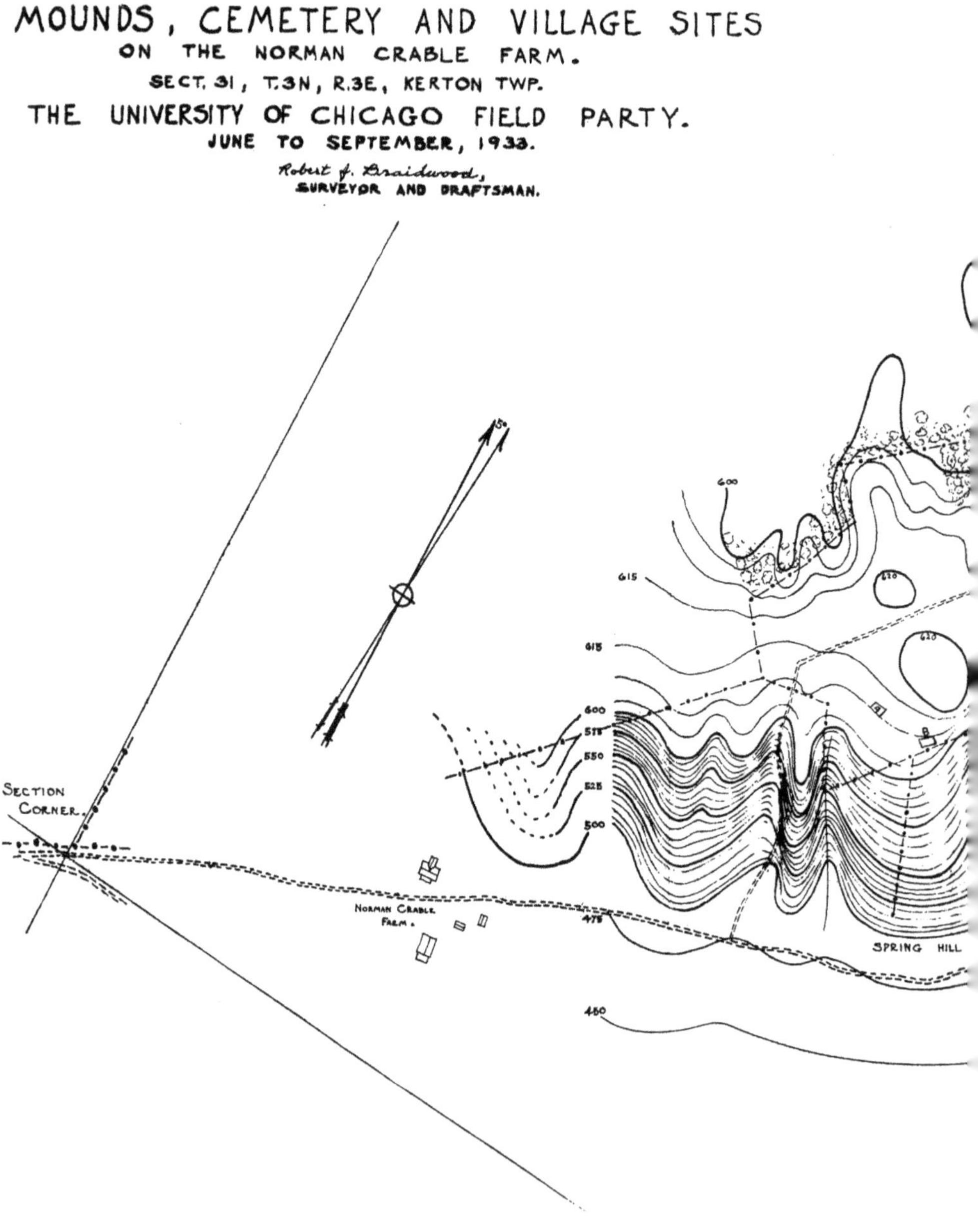
MOUNDS, CEMETERY AND VILLAGE SITES
ON THE NORMAN CRABLE FARM.
SECT. 31, T.3N, R.3E, KERTON TWP.
THE UNIVERSITY OF CHICAGO FIELD PARTY.
JUNE TO SEPTEMBER, 1933.
Robert J. Braidwood,
SURVEYOR AND DRAFTSMAN.
SECTION CORNER.
NORMAN CRABLE FARM.
SPRING HILL
600
615
620
620
615
600
575
550
525
500
475
480

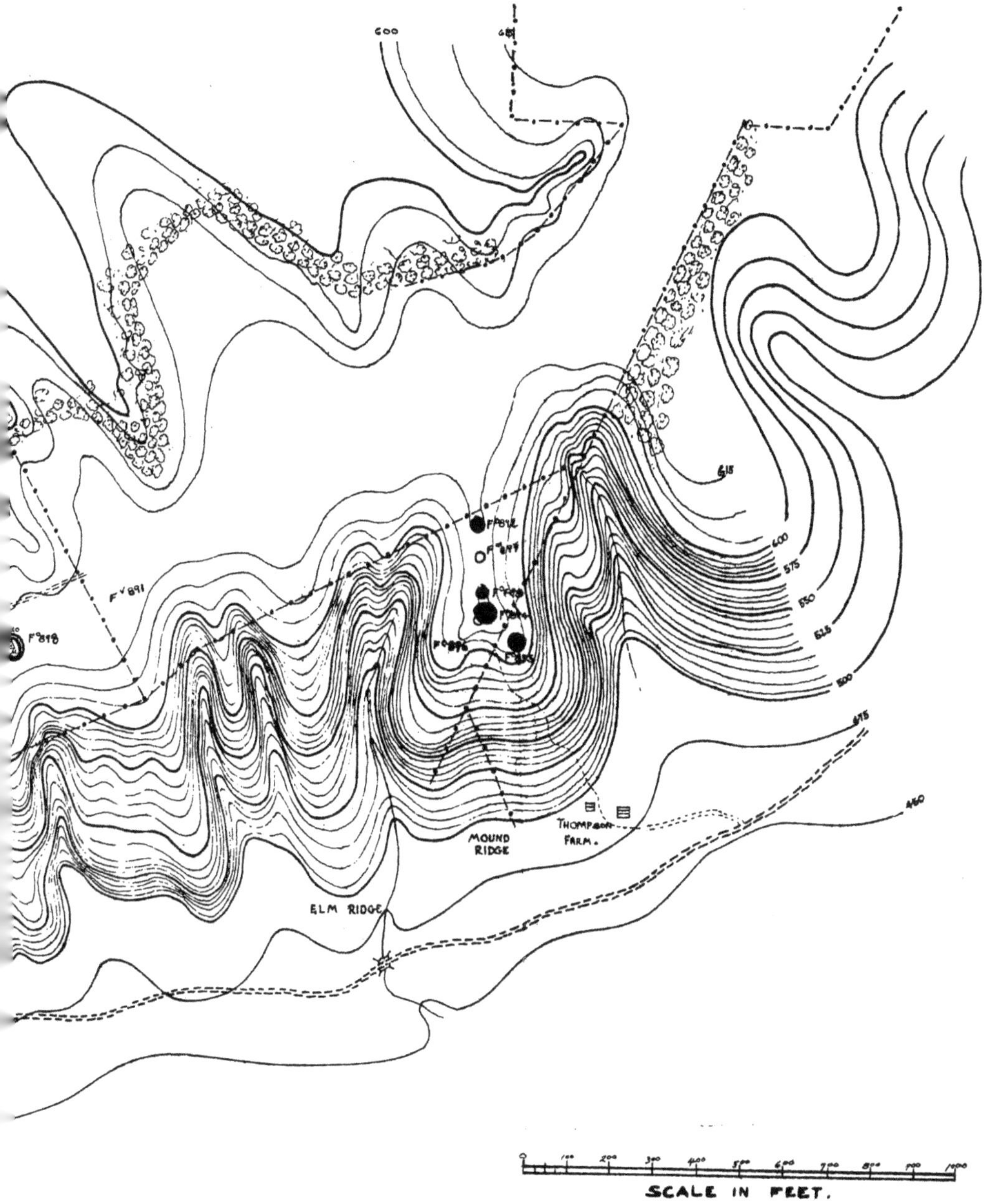
MOUND RIDGE
THOMPSON FARM.
ELM RIDGE
600
575
550
525
500
475
450
615
SCALE IN FEET.

SCALE 1" = 250'

Excavation of Pit A

In the excavation of pits A and B each area was staked off in 5-foot squares, and the material found was designated by the .4-foot level in which it was found. A circular refuse pit was encountered in Pit A, the upper part of which had apparently been used as a fireplace, for burned discolorations were noted near the top. The pit, which was 1.8 feet in diameter, contained charcoal, burned clay, shell, flint chips, Crable Plain, Crable Trailed, and Crable Cord-Marked pottery types. This pit occurred at a depth of 1.0 foot from the original surface level.

Around the pit and under the humus layer, which contained Oneota and Spoon River sherd types, shells, and flint chips, a sterile loess was encountered. This contained concretions, even at a depth of 0.5 foot. The presence of secondary lime deposits here, along with an extremely shallow humus and artifact zone, suggests that the surface had been lowered by erosion or by other forces. It is possible that this soil was removed for use in the erection of mound Fo898, which lies a short distance to the northeast.

Excavation of Pit B

A deeper deposit of cultural material was found in Pit B. This circumstance may have been due to a number of factors: first, it was located on the last level terrace above the steep slope of the bluff and would therefore tend to collect all materials washed down from the upper levels; second, it was at the edge of the cultivated field and would tend to retain such material as the process of cultivation and the consequent accelerated erosion displaced; third, the deposit may have been deeper in aboriginal times.

In square 1 of Pit B were Crable Plain, Crable Trailed, Crable Deep Rimmed Plate, and Crable Cord-Marked pottery types, shells, animal and fish bones, charred corncobs, shell hoes, a polished bone tube, and refuse pits. When the floor of Level 10 was cleared, three roughly circular pits were discovered that stood out distinctly from the loess. Each was about

TABLE I

Sherd Count of All Sherds from Fv891

		Large Jar Rim		Small Jar Rim			
		Flaring	Vertical	Flaring	Vertical	Shallow Bowl	Inde- terminate Shape
Crable Cord Marked	Rim	18	4	1	4	44	10
	Handles	4	4	4	0	0	1
	Body	0	24	0	0	1	405
Crable Plain	Rim	17	19	1	14	117	35
	Handles	2	3	0	3	0	0
	Body	0	3	0	0	1	404
Crable Trailed	Trailed	4	3	0	2	2	42
	Incised	2	0	0	0	6	13
	Punctate	2	2	0	0	2	10
	Hor. Pun.	1	4	0	0	3	6
	Ob. Or. Tr. Inc.	1	1	0	1	9	1
Wells Incised	Rim						
	Body						
	Trailed						
	Incised						
	Punctate						
	Hor. Pun.						
	Ob. Or. Tr. Inc.						
	Burnish						
Bell Plain		1				6	23
Tippet Bean Pot	Rim						
	Body						
	Handle						
Crable Deep Rimmed Plate	Rim						
	Body						
	Incised						
	Punctate						
	Burnish						
Kerton Incised							
Maples Mills							14
Spindle Whorls							
St. Clair Plain	Effigy heads					2	

TABLE I (Cont.)

Miniature Vessels	Shallow Plate	Intermediate Plate	Deep Plate	Beaker	Vessel	Spindle Whorl	Total	Per Cent
0								
3							535	27.92
0								
0								
12							1,104	57.62
0								
0								
0								
0							107	05.58
0								
0								
	36	1						
	8	1						
	14	1						
	28	1						
	5	0					97	05.00
	0	0						
	1	0						
	1	0						
							30	01.56
				9				
				2			12	00.62
				1				
			5					
			1					
			6				14	00.72
			1					
			1					
					1		1	00.05
							14	00.72
						2	2	00.10
							2	00.10
							1,916	99.99

2 feet in diameter and was circular in shape.[11] These pits contained the same type of cultural materials and animal remains as that found in the upper levels of Pit B. In the loess surrounding the pits only lime concretions occurred. The pits ended 4.8 feet from the surface. It is important to note that a sherd of Crable Deep Rimmed Plate was found in this lower level (Level 10). The particular decoration of this sherd consists of punctates outlining incised triangles.

In square 2 of Pit B, aside from the type of material found in square 1, there were small triangular projectile points of the characteristic Middle Mississippi type, a split bone awl, a worked core of a Busycon shell, abrading stones, hammerstones, red ochre, and shell spoons. In Level 6 were a few Maples Mills sherds in association with Crable Cord-Marked and Crable Plain sherds and a Middle Mississippi type projectile point. Two more ash pits occurred at a depth of 3.2 to 4.2 feet. In square 3 was a refuse pit in which was found the skull of a deer with its antlers attached.

The material from all levels of Pit B is rather homogeneous and evenly distributed. It is probably true that the upper 1.5 feet were added by erosion or by other factors already mentioned as irregular streaks of foreign soil appear above this level, and refuse pits do not occur until the lower part of Level 4.

Areas discolored by fire and containing small oval-shaped depressions occur at random over the village site. At present the function of these depressions is questionable, as they have not been excavated. (The cultural materials from Fv891 are illustrated on Plate I a - x. Table I gives the sherd count from Fv891.)

The Mound Group

This group is composed of four mounds, Fo892, Fo893, Fo894, and Fo895, and a large fire pit, Fm897, all of which are situated

[11] At Level 9 there was no evidence to indicate that there had been more than one ash pit. This feature was also found by the University of Chicago excavations at Starved Rock, Illinois, in a historic site and in excavations by the Museum of Anthropology, University of Michigan, at the protohistoric Mocassin Bluff site in Berrien County, Michigan. Both sites contain cultural materials which have affinities to Oneota and Fisher.

on a single axis forming a straight line along the spur of the bluff east of the excavated part of the village site. Mound Fo895 is a little off this axis, being somewhat southeast of the other mounds. (This mound was excavated by a local amateur archaeologist. As yet he has not located anything in it.) All the mounds were of the low, conical type built as superstructures to subfloor pit burials.

Mound Fo892

Mound Fo892 is directly adjacent to the village area and is 30 feet in diameter. The mound was slightly pitted by earlier diggers, but nothing has been reported found by them. The ridge is fairly heavily wooded, and some of the trees growing on the mounds are quite large. Their age is not great enough, however, to give any important information as to the date of the mound.

Before the construction of the mound the surface humus had been removed from all but the center of the site, where the old sod line was easily distinguished in the profile. After the humus was cleared, a small mound was built (2.5 feet high at the time of excavation). The soil used in the construction was a homogeneous mixture of humus and weathered loess. There was no evidence of a fire level, a prepared floor, a sand line, or any other type of preparation of the mound floor aside from the partial clearing off of the original humus layer. This mound was apparently constructed over the two burials which occurred in the center of it. The aboriginal burial pits (Features II and III) were both sunk from the original sod level to a depth of 3.0 feet. One burial occurred 4.2 feet from the present surface of the mound, while the other was at a depth of 5.0 feet (Pl. II*a*).

Burial I, Feature II, was in a bell-shaped pit; that is, the bottom of the pit was wider than the top. This is not true of Burial II, which was in a parallel-sided pit. An analysis of the 20-foot profile shows that the origin of Feature III is slightly higher than Feature II, with Feature II extending deeper than Feature III. All the evidence points to the fact that Feature II was dug and refilled after the mound structure was started. Before long Feature III was sunk through the same stratum that overlay Feature II. The mound was then completed.

Both skeletons lay extended at the bottom of their respectiv pits (Feature II and Feature III). The bodies were unaccompanied by grave goods, although a trace of red ochre on the bones indicates that they may have been smeared with paint prior to interment. Burial I, Feature II, was a female 45 to 50 years old; the hands were extended at the sides with the legs parallel and the head resting on the left side. The burial in Feature III was in such bad condition that it could not be measured or removed.

Fragments of charcoal, flint chips, red ochre, sherds, fire-cracked stones, and broken projectile points were scattered at random throughout the fill of the mound. From the whole moun only eleven sherds and three fragments of triangular projectile points were obtained.

The sherds are all badly weathered with the shell temperin leached out. Nine of the sherds are Crable Plain. Two sherds, not now available, were listed in the field notes as having a red slip on the exterior with a paste texture the same as Cahokia Red Filmed. One rim sherd, from a vertical-rimmed jar, has a handle attached, and was described in the field notes as "rim sherd with handle attached, of black laminated paste, brownish slip, shell tempered." This sherd seems to be of the same basic type as the others in the mound, although it may be of the Cahokia Red Filmed variety.

Depression Fm897

This depression was on the mound ridge between Fo892 and Fo893. It appeared on the surface before excavation as a well-defined, depressed area, much like a house plan. Just below the sod line bits of charcoal occurred and continued to be found down to the floor of the feature. Red burned earth appeared at a depth of 1.5 feet, following a well-defined line and having a regularity of width and direction. This structure was 10.5 feet long and 7 feet wide.

In square 110 at a depth of 1.3 feet a cluster of limestones lay, around which black claylike soil occurred. At the 1.5-foot level the rectangular red burned-clay rim showed distinctly in the yellow clay or weathered loess, the rim averaging 0.4 foot in width. The whole structure was oriented in a southeast and northwest direction. The excavators made a test of firing the weathered loess and found that when burned it turned the reddi color here mentioned.[12] The outside of the rim was very shallow, descending only 0.3 to 0.4 foot into the ground below the first point of observance. It also curved inward toward the center, being less broad at the base than at the point of discovery. The inside of the rim also curved in at the base and extended under the region enclosed by the burned clay. The latter was filled with charcoal, black shalelike stone, bits of limestone, and ashy soil. The red burned area did not extend beneath the entire rock-covered area. The stones on the floor were imbedded in a black "tarlike" crumbly soil. The soil beneath was in some places the natural loess and in others the burned red loess.

This feature was probably not a house structure — no post holes nor any evidence of a superstructure were found — but rather a large fire pit, prepared by scooping out a shallow basin and making a floor of black soil. It may be judged from the position of Fm897 that this fire pit had some ceremonial use; the exact function, however, is unknown.

The pottery and artifacts in the excavation of Fm897 were few. One Crable Plain sherd occurred in square 115L1. In square 105L1 there was a Cahokia Red Filmed sherd, the temper of which had been leached out. A Crable Plain rim sherd from a flaring rimmed jar was found in square 110L1 at a depth of 0.5 foot; the tempering had been leached out from this piece also. A snub-nosed scraper was found on the floor of the fire pit, a scraper with one side secondarily chipped, a blunt-nosed scraper, a granite abrading stone, and a piece of a slate pendant occurred on top of the south rim of the red-fired loess.

From what little evidence there is, Fm897 seems to belong to the Mississippi occupation period, as this structure does not yield the type of cultural material found around the Maples Mills fire pits which were discovered under the mounds and in the cemetery.

Mound Fo893

Mound Fo893 is 150 feet southeast of Fo892. It is a small mound, adjacent to Fo894 and 125 feet from Fm897. The peripheries of Fo893 and Fo894 tend to overlap or touch. Beyond Fo894 lies Fo895.

[12] Field notes by Thorne Deuel.

Mound Fo893, which was low and conical, was only partly excavated. A fire pit contained burned bones. This pit is on the original ground level and is of the same type as that found under Fo894, that is, it appears to be the remains of an old Maples Mills camp site. Before the mound was constructed, a pit was dug beside the fire pit, possibly for a burial, since a few skull fragments were found in it. The rest of the skeleton may have disintegrated, as the tree roots in the area have destroyed many of the other burials. When the pit was originally dug, material from the Woodland fire pit apparently slipped into the hole. One grit-tempered sherd was in the fill, which had been gathered up from the surface when the pit was refilled.

Mound Fo894

This conical mound, the largest of the group, was badly pitted by the local collectors; fortunately these pits were of a haphazard nature and so did not disturb all the burials in the mound. Tree roots also had destroyed some of the features. The overlapping of the edges of Fo893 and Fo894 may have been due to erosion which washed material from the top of the mounds, filling the space between the two structures. The sod was apparently removed before the building of the mound, as no old sod line was visible in the excavation. The profile shows a top layer of forest humus capping the mound fill, which in turn rests on weathered loess — the original ground surface minus the old humus line. At random throughout the fill of the mound were flint chips, remains of deer, fish, and human bones, fire-cracked stones, Mississippi and Woodland sherds, red ochre and charcoal, also one Woodland-like projectile point.

The mound was build over twelve burials. The majority of these were in pits dug from the original surface level, all being more or less uniform in depth. All the burials but one were extended (Fo894-6 was flexed) and were oriented to all angles of the main axis. There was a noticeable lack of grave goods as compared with the burials taken from the cemetery by McGirr.

A list of the burials and associated materials follows:

Fo894-1. Adult male. On the sternum was a shell gorget (Pl. III*a*).

Fo894-2. Adult male. Near the skull was a knife fragment, between the knees a graver (Pl. III*e*), a Maples Mills sherd one inch above the pelvis, and red ochre on the right femur.

Fo894-3. Infant. The upper half of the burial had been disturbed by a local collector's pit. A Cahokia Red Filmed sherd and a Maples Mills sherd were found in association.

Fo894-4. Adult female. The skull shows frontal cradleboard flattening. Two bone needles, circular in cross section, were close to the skull (Pl. 31).

Fo894-5. Infant. Above the burial were unworked river shells, Maples Mills, Crable Trailed, Crable Plain, and Crable Cord-Marked sherds.

Fo894-6. Adult (sex?). This was a flexed burial, interred during the construction of the mound. There was no evidence of its being in a pit, as over the burial lay soil apparently homogeneous with the rest of the mound fill. This burial lay nearer to the surface than did the others, being only 2.3 feet below the surface. Associated with it was a flint graver.

Fo894-7. Infant. The bones were so scattered that they could not be saved. The burial appears to have been placed in the mound after it was completed, but this cannot be stated positively, as there was a collector's pit near by which may have caused disturbance.

Fo894-8. No burial was given this number.

Fo894-9. Adult male. Associated with it was a pointed piece of elk antler, some charcoal, and a hammerstone.

Fo894-10. Infant. This body was badly disturbed by a local collector's pit.

Fo894-11. Infant. Also disturbed by a local collector's pit.

Fo894-12. Human mandible from the surface of the mound.

Fo894-13. Adult (sex?). Close to the right femur were two small triangular projectile points (Pl. IIIi).

Three fire pits were above the original ground level. Around these pits were Maples Mills sherds, fragments of deer bones and antlers, charcoal, burned clay, fire-cracked stones, Woodland-like projectile points, fish bones, and river shells. This material strongly suggests that at a time before the mounds were built a village site or camp of the Maples Mills group was located here. Possibly there is some correlation between the Maples Mills remains here and those of a village site with similar material below the bluffs. A Maples Mills village or camp site on this spur of the bluff would explain the presence of the Maples Mills sherds and occasional Woodland-like projectile points found throughout the fill of the mounds and in the village site at Crable. As the people who constructed the mounds gathered the dirt for the mound fill, the surface sherds, both Maples Mills and Mississippian, would be taken up and subsequently would occur sporadically throughout the mound.

Seventy-one sherds were taken from Fo894, 60 per cent of which are Maples Mills; the remaining 40 per cent belong to the Mississippi peoples. Two Woodland-type projectile points were also in the mound fill. The Middle Mississippi traits are: extended burials in pits, small triangular projectile points, bone needles, a shell gorget, cut shell spoons, and shell rattles. Other artifacts include the base of a stemmed projectile point, a stemmed projectile point, an abrading stone, and a hammerstone (Pl. III).

The Cemetery Fc896

The cemetery which the University of Chicago excavated was southwest of the mound group along the edge of the bluff. Twenty seven burials were removed, all of which were extended. Other cemeteries have been reported on other spurs of the bluff bordering the village site, but no work has been done in those areas. The cultural material with the burials was very meager as compared with the material taken out of the same cemetery by McGirr, a local farmer (Pl. XIa).

The burials lay at an average depth of 2.5 feet from the surface and had no fixed position of orientation. Three Maples Mills fire pits were in the cemetery area. Throughout this area, as in the mounds, occurred sporadic grit-tempered Maples Mills sherds. One of the Woodland fire pits, at a depth of 3.5 feet, contained Maples Mills sherds, a bone harpoon,[13] burned clay, broken deer bones, fish bones, ashes, mussel shells, and flint chips. Near the pit was a piece of cut antler, a Crable Plain sherd, and a small triangular projectile point (Middle Mississippi type). The Woodland fire pit was of the same type as that found under the mounds. Sixty feet away from the first fire pit was another 1.2 feet from the surface. In and around it were large Gooden Cord-Impressed[14] sherds, deer antlers,

[13] This harpoon is like Type I from the Fisher site (J. W. Griffin, 1946). Harpoons are also found in Grand River Focus sites.

[14] Cole and Deuel, *op. cit.*, p. 48. This type is referred to as Type 5 in this publication.

shells, stones, granite hammerstones, burned bone, a point of a deer bone awl, and fire-cracked stones. All this material was covered with wood ashes and humus. There was, however, not much indication of any firing of the loess below the ashes. No stratigraphy was noticed above the fire pit.

The burials of Fc896 and their associated materials are listed as follows:

Fc896-1. Adult male. This burial had occipital flattening. Associated with it was a small triangular projectile point.

Fc896-2. Infant. A Maples Mills Cord-Marked sherd was in association but probably got into the fill with the burial when it was covered.

Fc896-3. Age (?), sex (?). The burial was extended, lying in a north and south axis with the head toward the south.

Fc896-4. Infant. A Crable Plain sherd was in close association (Pl. IIb).

Fc896-5, 6. These were adult burials lying on either side of Fc896-4 (Pl. IIb).

Fc896-7. Infant. There are no data in the field notes on this burial, but small shell beads were mentioned in association with it.

Fc896-8. No data.

Fc896-9. There are no data on the skeleton itself. In the right hand of the body was a flint knife showing a little secondary chipping. In the left hand was a flake scraper with secondary chipping on the end and two sides. Also in association were deer bones and a Crable Trailed sherd.

Fc896-10. There are no data on the skeleton itself. This burial lay on a north and south axis with the head toward the south. Under the right ribs was a flint knife with coarse secondary chipping. Beneath the fourth rib on the left side was a small triangular projectile point. Over the skull were the remains of a small carnivore not further identified in the notes, and over the ribs was a Crable Plain sherd.

Fc896-11. This burial was extended. The arms, though extended, formed a greater angle with the trunk than is usual in burials in this position. Around the ankles were thirty-two pairs of mussel-shell rattles. The rattle was composed of a concave shell and a flat shell which was fitted onto the base. Holes were drilled or cut on each side of each shell to permit stringing. Inside were several pebbles which completed the rattle. Also, around the ankles occurred charcoal, corn, and burned clay (Pl. IVa).

Fc896-12. Adult female. The burial was extended, with the skeleton of a child (Fc896-17) lying on the pelvic region. Two unworked shells lay near the shoulder of Fc896-12. This burial was approximately 2 feet from the surface, lying in a north-south direction with the head toward the sout

Fc896-13. Infant. No data.

Fc896-14. Adult female, extended. A large, white chert knife was in the right hand.

Fc896-15. Nothing but loose bone in a collector's pit.

Fc896-16. Infant. No data.

Fc896-17. Infant, extended. The head was oriented toward the south. A Crable Trailed sherd was in association.

Fc896-18, 19, 20. These were simply loose bones in a collector's pit.

Fc896-21. No data.

Fc896-22. No data on the skeleton itself. A large, white chert knife was in the left hand; the knife had secondary chipping on one edge.

Fc896-23. This burial was extended in an east-west direction; the head was toward the west. The third and fourth lumbar vertebrae were fused. A bone ring was in association with the skull. Near the vertex of the skull lay a fragment of a large chipped blade of chert.

Fc896-24. No data as to the sex or age are available. Above the left patella were 8 triangular side-notched projectile points that are similar to points found at Cahokia Mound.[15] Also near the left patella was a cut tip of a deer tine with a shallow groove encircling the larger end. Associated with the right foot was a Crable Plain sherd.

Fc896-25. Infant. This burial was oriented in an east-west direction with the head toward the west. At the left elbow was a small two-handled Crable Plain jar with the interior painted red. Inside the jar was an uncut valve of a river mollusk.

Fc896-26. Infant. This burial lay across the knees of burial Fc896-2

Fc896-27. Infant. Oriented in an east-west direction with the head toward the west.

Fc896-28. Adult male. An extended burial oriented in an east-west direction with the head toward the west. A small Crable Plain jar without loop handles was in association. This vessel was above the left knee and close to Fc896-25 (Pl. IV*b*).

[15] Titterington, 1938, Figs. 9 and 10.

Fc896-29. Infant. An extended burial with the body oriented in an east-west direction. The head lay on the left femur of Fc896-28 (Pl. IVb).

Fc896-30. Adult female. This burial was extended in a north-south direction.

Fc896-31. Only the lower extremities were in place; the rest of the body was disturbed by local collectors.

Fc896-32. Isolated skull.

Loose in the fill throughout the cemetery were polished bone tubes, small, circular, ground-shell beads, Crable Plain, Crable Cord-Marked, Crable Trailed, Crable Deep Rimmed Plate, Wells Incised, St. Clair Plain, and Maples Mills sherds, triangular projectile points, and charcoal. In one aboriginal pit were a small St. Clair Plain water bottle, animal bones, six perforated mussel shells, and an abrading stone.

One skull (Fc896-101), taken from the cemetery by McGirr, was reported by George Neumann[16] as showing evidences of scalping. Neumann said: "Here, then, there is direct evidence of a case of scalping of an individual who belonged to a group with a Middle Mississippi culture that was shown in Illinois to be prehistoric and by relative chronology to postdate Hopewellian manifestations."[17] On the other hand, he also stated: "The only other case of direct evidence for scalping that the writer has encountered was in a skull from the Madisonville cemetery, a Fort Ancient Aspect site that shows white contact and therefore does not indicate any antiquity as far as scalping is concerned."[18] He stated further that scalping was unknown until comparatively recent times among the Siouan-speaking tribes of the Plains: ". . . that is, it was quite common at the time the whites came in contact with them."[19]

From the above evidence and from the conclusions concerning the Madisonville cemetery, a similar conclusion might be

[16] Neumann, 1940.
[17] Ibid., p. 287.
[18] Ibid., p. 288.
[19] Ibid., p. 289.

drawn for Crable, for although no positive evidence of white contact is present, it will be shown in this report that Crable is a relatively late site. When Neumann's article was written, Crable was thought to be exclusively a Middle Mississippi site of some antiquity, but, as will be pointed out, Crable is a mixed site of Upper and Middle Mississippi affiliations. The Upper Mississippi influences at Crable are Oneota and may, therefore, be close to the historic Siouan,[20] Iowa, Missouri, and Oto tribes. The evidence leads one to believe, therefore, that scalping occurred at Crable at a comparatively late date. Scalping is noted also at the McFate site in northwestern Pennsylvania at a late date.[21]

A DESCRIPTION OF THE MATERIAL FROM THE MCGIRR COLLECTION[22]

For a number of years prior to 1933, Mr. Glenn McGirr, a local resident, periodically dug at the Crable site. A collection of the cultural material which he found is now housed in the Dickson Mound State Park, Lewiston, Illinois.

Bone artifacts include pins, fish hooks, antler pressure flakers, awls, a thong stropper, and rings. The fish hooks are unbarbed and have a groove around the shank end. Two bone pins were found, one with a rounded top part and two rounded sections below it, the other decorated with a carved design resembling a conventionalized human head (Pl. Vj-m, w-z, a', b').

Shell artifacts include spoons cut like the typical Fulton County Middle Mississippi ones (Plate XIIa). Various pendants are present, the majority circular with one, two, or four perforations. One pendant is rectangular with three perforations. A circular pendant has scalloped edges with two holes for suspension. Two circular pendants, one with scalloped edges, have a cross design made by cutting out areas of the shell. One

[20] J. B. Griffin, 1937.

[21] Personal communication from J. B. Griffin based on photographs from the Pennsylvania Historical Commission.

[22] Mr. Donald Dickson, in a personal communication, stated that all of the material in the McGirr Collection came from Fc896.

unique incised circular shell bears the cross and stepped "cloud design." The stepped cloud motif is reminiscent of vessel designs from the southeastern Missouri-northeastern Arkansas area. This particular piece does not have any perforations. One pendant has an incised spider design and two perforations for suspension. Snail-shell beads with their bases ground off and holes made on either side for suspension are present. Circular ground-shell beads about one-fourth inch in diameter are also found. Shell hoes and rattles, such as are described in connection with burial Fo896-11, occur in numbers (Pl. V*a*, *b*, *r*-*v*, *c*'-*k*').

Copper artifacts include beads of rolled copper, triangular stemmed projectile points, and copper-covered wooden ear spools.

The stone complex includes small, triangular projectile points and small, stemmed and notched projectile points, many with no secondary chipping. Flint-shouldered awls, two equal-armed pipes, a smoothed calcite rod, a shale pendant of a willow-leaf shape having one hole for suspension, a flint mace ten inches long, a stone hoe,[23] a biconcave discoidal, two celts, and two grooved club heads make up the worked-stone artifacts found by McGirr (Pl. V *c*-*i*, *o*-*p*).

The bone, shell, and stone artifacts are for the most part of the same type as the material gathered by the University of Chicago at Crable and other Middle Mississippian sites in the Fulton County area. A few exotic pieces stand out as unique for the area: the flint mace and the incised shell pendants which are related to the rest of the Southern Cult materials found at Crable.

Two clay equal-armed elbow pipes and one clay pottery trowel are in the collection (Pl. V*n*, *q*).

The pottery found by McGirr is about equally divided between pieces of typical Spoon River Focus and the Oneota Aspect with or without the Southern Cult designs. There are also trade pieces from the south that probably have a relationship to the Southern Cult materials.

Eighteen St. Clair Plain effigy bowls are in the collection. These bowls are rather low and rounded and have a bird or animal head attached to the lip on one side of the bowl; on the other side is a projection representing a conventionalized tail. In the

[23] Similar to one figured by Titterington, 1938, Fig. 18.

majority of the bowls the head faces outward, but in three cases the head is facing back over the bowl. Some of the bowls have an effigy bird head with a comblike projection on the top. These bowls occur with or without side lugs which appear to be conventionalized wings. This kind of bowl is typical of the sort found in Spoon River sites. Two bowls, instead of the projecting head, have an effigy of the face of an owl molded into the shoulder of the vessel. The shoulder curves inward; the head occurs on the top side of one end and the tail at the other (Pl. VI a, c-j).

The St. Clair Plain water bottles have either short, wide necks or long, slender ones. One relatively wide-mouthed water bottle 5 3/4 inches high has fifteen lobes evenly spaced around the body. The lobes begin at the shoulder and extend to the base. The outside convex lobes are concave on the interior (Pl. VII g). There are two St. Clair Plain blank-faced effigy bottles present. The larger bottle has the capacity of approximately one quart; the smaller is a miniature about 3 1/2 inches high.

The Crable Trailed and Crable Plain shallow bowls are represented by thirty-seven specimens. These occur with and without lugs. Some are plain; others are decorated. The lugs are "eared," semilunar, or scalloped. There are one, two, three, or four lugs, equally distant from one another. Decoration occurs generally in the region of the lip and rim. This type of vessel is also found in Spoon River sites, the slight difference being the type of design present and its frequency, which points to Oneota influence. There are five miniature jars having the capacity of one to two ounces, which have flaring rims and are carefully decorated. One shows a circle with a cross inside; the other, a chevron design. These miniature jars occur with or without handles.

A unique piece is a compound vessel having two bowls joined by a central bar; each of the outer rims carries a handle groove down the center. This vessel is 10 inches long and 3 1/2 inches high (Pl. VII f).

A Cahokia Red Filmed water bottle, a negative painted water bottle (Pl. VII e), two Kerton Incised water bottles, two Bell Plain water bottles, and an Old Town Red bottle occur. One cord-marked water bottle is present and is atypical of this group. Another water bottle has a wide mouth and is decorated with red painted circles within each of which is a plain, painted cross. These circles occur in two bands around the vessel. A water bottle with a neck of medium length has a triangular appliqué clay band just below the neck on the shoulder; this encircles the smooth surface of the vessel at a slight angle. This bottle is similar to some Arkansas water bottles illustrated by Harrington.[24]

Eight Tippets Bean Pots occur.

The jars (forty-two examples) and plates (twenty-two examples) in the McGirr Collection conform to those discussed in the following section on pottery types. It is, however, interesting to note that no shallow bowls were found by McGirr. The Crable Deep Rimmed Plate is the only plate form represented.

A problematical grit-tempered piece identical with a piece from Kingston Lake was found. This is a conical vessel with two projections that might be called legs at the base of the cone (Pl. VII d).

Two of the vessels in the collection are exact duplicates, but one is shell tempered and the other grit tempered. The rim outline is roughly oval and the base conical. Both of the specimens are cord-marked. The shape of these two vessels is similar to the forms found in late Woodland sites of the area. No data as to their association in Fc896 are available. These two pieces do not tie in with any other material from the site.

POTTERY TYPES FOUND AT CRABLE

The following is a classification and description of all the pottery types found at Crable, including the material excavated by the University of Chicago and the pottery in the McGirr Collection.

Crable Plain

Paste:

Temper: The temper is of shell, either coarse or medium, and is visible from the surface.

Texture: Coarse to medium, the shell tempering is scattered irregularly through the vessel and occurs at all angles in relation to the surface of the vessel. The

[24] Harrington, 1920, Plate LXXXV.

sherd fractures transversely, and the paste is often laminated when viewed in cross section. The clay also tends to be rough and occurs in whorls.

Hardness: 2-3.

Color:

Exterior: Uneven firing caused the color to vary, so the pottery runs from a light gray to a reddish gray to dark brown. Some sherds are of a reddish color throughout, due to the firing of the vessel in an oxidizing atmosphere, the thinness of the vessel, and the iron in the clay itself.

Interior: The interior of the pottery is similar in color to the exterior, but is generally darker. The colors are red, terra cotta, and tan. Some are badly smudged; a few are burnished. The core is sometimes gray.

Surface Finish:

The outside surface has either been roughly scraped, leaving pieces of clay nodules still clinging to the vessel, or has been finely smoothed. Some of the vessel surfaces are burnished. The surface on the roughly finished pieces has rough, irregular scars on both the interior and exterior of the vessel. The interior of the vessel generally has been smoothed down more than the exterior. In a very few sherds the interior has been painted red.

Form:

Shallow bowls:

Rim: straight, usually 1 or 2 mm. thicker than the body of the bowl.

Body: circular, thickness from 5 to 12 mm.

Base: rounded.

Appendages: none except for occasional lobing of the lip.

Jars: Large, small, and medium. Rim diameter runs from 6 to 12 inches (Pl. VIII d, i).

Rim: Variations occur from marked flaring to vertical rim. Wide and medium wide mouthed. Handles occur; either two, three, or four attached to the lip and the body. They are rounded or elliptical in cross section. The width is constant between these attachments. The handles are attached by riveting or welding. In some cases the construction of such a handle caused a widening of the lip of the vessel. The handle may have a pair of ornamental nodes at its top with or without a groove on the exterior surface of the handle and between the nodes (Pl. VI m-t, w-y).

Lips: These are generally unmodified by thickening, although the larger specimens may have a thickened lip.

Body: The body is globular or hemispherical and has a somewhat flattened bottom.

Crable Cord-Marked

The temper, texture, hardness, color, surface finish, and forms are the same for this type as for Crable Plain. The presence of cord-marking on the exterior of the vessel distinguishes this type from Crable Plain. A few sherds show that the cord-marking was occasionally smoothed over. The interiors of the vessels are treated in the same manner as those of the Crable Plain except that they are sometimes red slipped or painted. On the cord-marked pieces no decoration occurs aside from the exterior cord-marking, which sometimes comes up to the lip, at other times only to the shoulder of the jar. The distance of the cord-marking from the lip is variable. Both the shallow bowls and the jar forms present are cord-marked (Pls. VIII f, XI b).

Crable Trailed

This type is distinguished from the Crable Plain only by the fact that it is decorated. The decorations occur on the lip, shoulder, and, in the case of the jars, body. On a few jars and bowls decorations occur inside the vessel near the lip. The decorations are composed of:

a. Trailing. Comparatively wide lines made with a blunt instrument while the clay was wet.
b. Incising. Narrower lines than the trailed type were executed by a sharper instrument while the clay was wet.
c. Punctates. Made with a hollow-tubed instrument, such as a reed.
d. Horizontal punctates. This type of decoration was made by a blunt-pointed instrument and occurs at the end of trailed lines or by itself in a series or in a pattern. The instrument was held at a slight angle (about 30 degrees) to the surface of the vessel and pushed into the clay while it was still wet (Pls. VI k-i, VIII a-c, e, g-h, j-o).

Crable Deep Rimmed Plate

Griffin[25] has described St. Clair Plain of the Cahokia area which is related to this type as well as to Crable Plain, although it does not carry the decorative tradition. Adams[26] has described the identical ware but has called it Imperial Plain. He stated: "The closest analogy to this ware is the 'dull gray ware' described on page 49 of Rediscovering Illinois..."

Paste:
- Temper: Shell temper from medium to fine and not as visible from the surface as in Crable Plain.
- Texture: Medium to fine with the shell temper distributed throughout the paste more evenly than in Crable Plain. The paste is homogeneous and well made. In a small percentage of the sherds the tempering material is not visible.
- Color: Black is predominant on the sherds, although shades of red and gray are common. The coloring of the exterior and the interior of the vessels is, for the most part, uniform.
- Hardness: 2.5-3.

Surface Finish:
The exterior surface is smoothed uniformly or is finely scraped. A small percentage of the vessels are burnished; these are similar to Powell Plain from the Cahokia area.

Decoration:
- Trailing: Same as for Crable Trailed.
- Incising: Same as for Crable Trailed
- Punctates: Same as for Crable Trailed.
- Postfired incising.

Form: Deep Plate.
Decoration covers all of the interior of the vessel except the bottom. The sides of the vessel are at a 45 degree angle to the base, with straight sides minus any lip thickening (Pls. VI a'-f', IX m-v, X d).

Wells Incised

This type is described by Griffin. The paste is the same as that of St. Clair Plain and Crable Deep Rimmed Plate. The surface

[25] J. B. Griffin, 1949.
[26] Adams, 1941.

finish and the technique of decoration are the same as for Crable Deep Rimmed Plate. This type represents the typical Middle Mississippi plate form of which two subgroups are discernible at Crable; the shallow plate and the intermediate plate (intermediate between the shallow plate and the Crable Deep Rimmed Plate). The decoration always occurs in the upper rim surface. The designs are composed of various elements: line-filled triangles with alternating blank triangular areas, oblique lines in groups, nested-parallel-semicircular lines bordered with small triangles, groups of parallel lines vertical to the base bordered with small triangles, and trailed oblique lines bordered with punctates and chevron designs (Pls. VI b, u, v, z; IX a-i; X m).

St. Clair Plain

This is a type described by Griffin.[27] It has the same paste tradition as Crable Deep Rimmed Plate and Imperial Plain.[28] At Crable the typical Middle Mississippi effigy bowls, blank-faced effigy bottles, a lobed vessel, and water bottles fall into this type. A water bottle with a triangular appliqué strip running obliquely around the body possibly also is of this type, although it may be classified as a probable Middle Mississippi type from eastern Arkansas (Pls. VI a, c-j; VII g).

Tippets Bean Pot

The bean pot has a straight or inslanting wall with a flat base. The horizontal rod handles are generally attached to the sides of the vessel midway between the base and the lip and at Crable are usually deer tine in shape. The handle with the hand appearing on the distal end is not found at Crable. The side opposite the handle has either an indented pouring spout at the lip level or has an attached lug. One specimen in the McGirr Collection has two lugs opposite each other. These pots are either painted red or are plain. It should be noted also that at Crable there is no decoration on the bean pot, such as incising or engraving.

[27] J. B. Griffin, op. cit.
[28] Adams, op. cit.

Griffin has best described this type.[29] It is analogous to the "bean pot vessel" referred to by Kelly and Cole.[30]

Kerton Incised

The paste of this type is like that of Crable Deep Rimmed Plate. Only three vessels were found at Crable. One is a vertical compound vessel from Fv891. Two loop handles are present. The body is decorated with trailed and punctate designs composed of an element that is reminiscent of the "weeping eye" design associated with the Southern Cult of the southeastern United States, and with Oneota curvilinear and punctate designs (Pl. I r).

The second is a wide-mouthed water bottle with incised cross and circle designs encircling the vessel in rows; between rows are two wavy incised lines. This vessel has a flattened base which also is decorated (Pl. VII a, b).

The third is a long, narrow-mouthed water bottle similar in decoration to the one described above. The decoration on Kerton Incised vessels is generally more ornate and geometric than on Crable Incised vessels, although it does not always show a refined technique in the application.

Cahokia Red Filmed

The paste of this ware is the same as that of St. Clair Plain. The surface is red slipped and sometimes has been subsequently polished. At Crable the forms carrying this red slip are water bottles and plates. This type is also described by Griffin.[31]

Bell Plain

Two vessels of this type (now in the McGirr Collection) occur at Crable. One is a tripod water bottle with a carinated body. The legs are globular and hollow; the neck is tall, projecting from the center of the body. This vessel is 8 1/2 inches high and the neck is 4 inches long. The body width is 7 1/4 inches (Pl. VII h). The other vessel is a tripod water bottle that has legs like the above vessel but a more globular body.

[29] J. B. Griffin, *op. cit.*
[30] Kelly and Cole, 1931.
[31] J. B. Griffin, *op. cit.*

Old Town Red[32]

One vessel of this type is in the McGirr Collection. This vessel has three large, globular, hollow legs that are attached by spouts to one common neck. This is a burnished red painted vessel (Pl. VII *c*).

A few fabric-impressed salt-pan sherds occur, having the simple "over one under one" technique.

Negative Painted

Only one water bottle shows evidence of negative painting at this site. The exterior surface of the vessel is of a reddish color, the result of firing in an oxidizing atmosphere, and has been painted black. The decorative motif of crosses and dots is spaced sporadically over the body. The neck is encircled by two parallel lines of small squares (Pl. VII *e*).

DISCUSSION OF THE CRABLE POTTERY TYPES

For the most part the ceramic complex at Crable follows that of the typical Middle Mississippi tradition in the Cahokia and Spoon River areas. There is, however, an Oneota element that distinguishes Crable from most other Middle Mississippi sites in the area. The typical Middle Mississippi types found at Crable include all of the above-named types except Crable Trailed, Crable Deep Rimmed Plate, Old Town Red, Wells Incised, Bell Plain, Negative Painted, and Kerton Incised, but even some of these have Middle Mississippi elements. All of these types are apparently roughly contemporaneous, with no indication of a time difference. In all the arbitrary stratigraphic levels, the various types except Bell Plain and Old Town Red are present. Crable Plain, Crable Cord-Marked, and Crable Trailed are the most abundant, while Wells Incised and Crable Deep Rimmed Plate are in the minority.

The Crable Deep Rimmed Plate is the only unique type occurring at Crable. These plates always have on the interior of the rim incised, trailed, or punctate designs of the Oneota style,

[32] Phillips, Ford, Griffin, 1949.

which also appear on the Crable Trailed vessels and sherds. It is of interest to note that no shallow plates (Wells Incised) were found by McGirr in his work in the cemetery. All the plates there were Crable Deep Rimmed Plate. In the village areas there were seven Wells Incised shallow plates to one Crable Deep Rimmed Plate. This may indicate that the deep plate was used more as a mortuary offering vessel and that the shallow plate was utilitarian. The Crable Deep Rimmed Plate type does not occur in "pure" Oneota sites. The decoration on this type is in the Oneota style; therefore, one infers that a transference of technique has taken place, probably indicating a cultural fusion from two separate sources.

Crable Trailed is decorated in a manner typical of the Oneota Aspect which has a series of decorative motifs characteristically found on jars. In Crable Trailed these features are also found on a few shallow bowls. The Lake Winnebago Focus has shallow bowls with lug handles. These differ from the Crable shallow bowls which do not have the lug handles and which are decorated.

Crable Cord-Marked differs in some respects from the Spoon River material. At Crable a very small amount of the Crable Cord-Marked has been smoothed over. Cord-marking is never combined with Oneota designs on the jars. Also, incised or trailed designs are never found on the shoulder when the cord-marking has been smoothed. At Crable a greater number of cord-marked sherds was found than at any other Middle Mississippi site in the area: 37.03 per cent of the sherds from Fv891 are Crable Cord-Marked.[33] Crable also has a larger amount of tempering material present with larger individual pieces than have other sites in the area. At Cahokia about 66 per cent of the cord-marked sherds have the interior painted red. At Crable only three cord-marked sherds are so painted. In form one sees that Cahokia Cord-Marked is made up predominantly of cooking jars, a Cahokia variant of a widespread Middle Mississippi shape.[34] Cord-marking at Crable occurs on both jars and shallow bowls. Trappist influences were felt earlier in the "pure" Spoon River Focus sites, but Cahokia Cord-Marked was not strong in this area.

The Crable Plain, which has a paste like that of St. Clair

[33] Titterington, 1938, Fig. 40<u>g</u>, Fig. 42<u>a</u>; J. B. Griffin, 1949.
[34] J. B. Griffin, 1949.

Plain,[35] differs from the latter type in that burnished sherds occasionally occur. This element may be a survival of the burnishing technique found in Powell Plain,[36] which is an Old Village Focus type found over an extensive area in the Middle and Upper Mississippi Valley. In the Peoria area Powell Plain is not present in sites in which there is a mixture of Middle Mississippi and Oneota. Griffin noted two divisions in Powell Plain: a polished and a dull surface treatment with the polished being the more predominant. The Crable Plain, on the other hand, has a predominance of dull surfaces but also differs in that the paste is like that of St. Clair Plain. It appears that Crable Plain and St. Clair Plain are a continuation and development of a technique that appeared in Old Village Focus times.

In the cemetery the jar and the deep plate make up 40.5 per cent of the vessels. Other pieces not typically Spoon River or Oneota make up 8.4 per cent of the vessels in the McGirr Collection. These pieces are typical of the Old Town Red and Bell Plain vessels from northeastern Arkansas, described by Moore.[37] A certain percentage of the shallow bowls occurring at Crable show a combination of features different from the Spoon River type of shallow bowl. These features are: incised, trailed or postfired incised decorations on the inside of the rim, oblique or transverse lip incising, and equally spaced paired-eared projections or lugs around the rim. This type of decoration is the same as that found on the jar and suggests that Oneota jar decoration was applied to other types of vessels. The plain shallow bowls are typical of the Spoon River Focus shallow bowls, as are the water bottles, bean pots, shallow and intermediate plates, and effigy bowls.

None of the vessels at Crable has the interlocking scroll design common on the shoulder of the jars at Cahokia, Old Village, Aztalan, and Middle Mississippi sites in Jo Daviess County, Illinois. The design on the vessel pictured in Plate VIII e is very similar to the design frequently seen on the jars from Mississippi sites in Jo Daviess County and Aztalan and may be indicative of some contact or connection between the two areas. Vessels from these two areas differ, however, in shape. The Crable jars do not have so acute an angle in the shoulder as do those of this type from northern Mississippi sites.

[35] Ibid.
[36] Ibid.
[37] Moore, 1910.

Designs typical of the Southern Cult are found only on Crable Trailed, Crable Deep Rimmed Plate, and Kerton Incised. The negative painted water bottle probably came from southeast Missouri and is part of the Southern Cult ceremonial expression.

CONCLUSIONS

The Crable Village site, cemetery, and mound group are contemporaneous, as the type of material found in all three places is very homogeneous. The fact that there was no stratigraphy and that the existing deposit was very shallow supports the belief that this group was of one unified complex, existing at the same time.

At Crable three cultural elements are present: Woodland, Spoon River (with definite Southern Cult influence), and Oneota. The latter two are mixed in the village, cemetery, and the mound group, while the former is regarded as a prior occupation.

The Maples Mills people used the area as a camp or village site before the later peoples arrived. Fire pits were found on the original ground level, and Maples Mills sherds in small amounts were found in the fill of the mounds. We also see the evidence of this group in the cemetery and under the mounds where fire pits with sherds are found.

This Woodland occupation occurred not long before the Mississippi occupation, as there was no accumulation of forest humus over the fire-pit area. It is possible that this area was a temporary camp site with some relationship to the Maples Mills site located about one-quarter mile east of the mound group.[38]

In the village area there was not as much evidence of the Woodland peoples as in the cemetery and under the mound group. Only fourteen Maples Mills sherds were found in the entire excavation of Fv891 by the University of Chicago, this number being 0.72 per cent of the total number of sherds. It is possible that the section of the village site excavated had been stripped of its surface soil in order to build Fo898, or there may have been no Woodland material in the area excavated. There is no

[38] Donald Wray in a personal communication reported this Woodland site.

evidence to lead one to believe that there was any sort of relationship between this group and the later Mississippi group. There is no developmental sequence from the Maples Mills to the Mississippi culture.

Cole and Deuel[39] believed that the Maples Mills Focus was influenced by the Mississippi culture, although it maintained an individuality of its own. At Crable we see that the two groups were not contemporaneous, as the Maples Mills was stratigraphically under the Mississippi occupation.

The Southern Cult was more common in the Southeast, but did spread over most of the Mississippi Valley. This "cult" is found in Middle Mississippi sites in the Southeast, but when it appears in the northern Mississippi Valley it is also associated with Upper Mississippi sites. It is interesting to note that the features which make up this cult are not found in Fulton County sites outside of Crable. This cult is characterized by certain features which have a high degree of similarity over its entire area. The material culture contains such items as conch-shell masks marked with the winged or "weeping eye" design, copper and shell pendants with repoussé circles and crosses or with the background cut out, shell gorgets showing fighting turkey cocks, spiders, or rattlesnakes, monolithic stone axes, large stone batons, circular paint palettes, and pottery engraved with the horned and winged rattlesnake.[40]

At Crable items to be associated with this cult are engraved shell gorgets and pendants with the cross and spider design, a chipped flint mace, and pottery decorations of the cross and circle. On one Kerton Incised vessel there is a weeping eye design.

The designs typical of the Southern Cult are found on Crable Trailed, Crable Deep Rimmed Plate, and Kerton Incised vessels. Crable Trailed, which is made up of jars and shallow bowls, is of a type closely related to the Oneota found in the Orr Focus of Iowa. At Crable, therefore, it is clearly indicated that these two influences, Southern Cult and Oneota, were contemporary. Titterington illustrated sherds from Cahokia that carry the cross and weeping eye design, showing that some Southern Cult influences were present there also.[41]

It is important to note that at Crable there was one occupation

[39] _Op. cit._, p. 192.
[40] Waring and Holder, 1945.
[41] _Op. cit._, Fig. 42, _f_, _g_.

aside from the earlier Maples Mills, yet we find that there was a complete mixture of two separate so-called phases: Upper and Middle Mississippi. From the evidence at hand one sees that the Spoon River sites are prehistoric, except for one excavation mentioned by Powell[42] at Lake Peoria. There are several Middle Mississippi sites in the area, however, which show that Oneota design elements and techniques were appearing to a smaller degree. At the sites Fv47 and Fv49, Crable Trailed-like jar sherds occur,[43] and in the Crabtree site[44] Oneota jars, circular shell spider gorgets, and northeastern Arkansas and southeastern Missouri vessel types are associated with a predominant number of Middle Mississippi traits.

In comparing Crable with other sites it is necessary to separate, as far as possible, the Oneota and the Middle Mississippi elements and to make a comparison on this basis. If one is to obtain a valid conception of this site, the culture complex must be viewed as a cultural whole. For comparative purposes the various elements have been separated in the traditional manner. It is, of course, difficult to evaluate some of the traits and to know into which division they fall. In such a site as Crable, where a mixture occurs, it is unwise to make a marked distinction in many of the cultural items as many traits are co-existent in both the Middle and Upper Mississippi phases.

The Middle Mississippi traits conform to the general Spoon River Focus sites in the area. It is clear that Crable's Spoon River materials have closer affiliations with late Cahokia (Trappist Focus) than with Old Village and Aztalan for the following reasons: the cord-marked pottery which is found so abundantly at Crable is apparently nonexistent at Aztalan but shows a relationship to the Cahokia Cord-Marked of the Trappist Focus; Powell Plain, associated with the Old Village manifestation and similar to Aztalan, is represented at Crable by only a few sherds. This situation does show some contemporaneity of Cahokia and Aztalan, as Bennett has shown to be true also in the Jo Daviess County sites.[45]

The Upper Mississippi elements at the site are fully developed

[42] Powell, 1894, p. 18.

[43] Data and some specimens in the Ceramic Repository for the Eastern United States.

[44] Snyder, 1908.

[45] Bennett, 1945, p. viii.

Oneota which were not developed here but were brought into this area. The extensive village site was occupied for a relatively short time, as the village area does not have a very deep occupational stratum and the refuse pits are not numerous. This indicates that a fairly large population was present during a short period. We find that a large population covering a wide area is one of the noticeable features of the Oneota people of Iowa. The presence of numerous snub-nosed scrapers also points to Oneota affiliations.[46] When one searches for areas from which the Oneota found at Crable could have come, one looks to the northwest and west.

The burial complex of the various foci of the Oneota Aspect is variable. In the Orr Focus of the Iowa Oneota, as at Crable, the burials are extended and grouped in cemeteries with grave goods of pottery and miscellaneous artifacts. Crable also has burials that occur in conical mounds. This type of burial is a feature of the Grand River Focus of Wisconsin and the Orr Focus sites of Minnesota. In Iowa the burials are also intrusive into mounds constructed by people of another culture. Also at Crable, as in the Grand River and Lake Winnebago foci, unspecialized pottery types occur with the burials, and, as in the Orr Focus, small, crude, funerary vessels are present with the burials. The Missouri Oneota, as shown at the Utz site, varies from this general pattern with the burials being haphazardly placed in the village area without ceramic grave goods. In the Blue Earth Focus of Minnesota, flexed burials occur in storage pits with pottery grave goods. The Leary site of Nebraska has primary, extended, supine, and secondary bundle burials at random in the village area with few grave goods, which never include pottery. Burials there are possible also in mounds. In the burial complex of the Fort Ancient Aspect all the traits found in the western variants of Upper Mississippi occur in the various foci, but it must be noted that most of the burial traits are present in all four of the Fort Ancient foci, and in addition cremation occurs in the Baum Focus.

The following are the nonpottery traits at Crable that "might be listed which seem to be characteristic of Oneota, particularly of the Orr Focus and closely related foci, but not of Fort Ancient: double pointed flint knife, the edge scraper, the pointed scraper, the end scraper; a somewhat smaller triangular

[46] McKern, 1931, p. 385.

arrowpoint; the Oneota type of arrow-shaft rubber, grooved maul, tanged shell spoon, copper implements and the copper tubular bead."[47]

The traits found at Crable, which are listed by Griffin[48] as characteristic of the Fort Ancient Aspect, but which do not seem to be common elements in the Oneota are: slate pendants,[49] the discoidal, the stone hoe, the drill with expanding base, side-notched arrow points, antler-section hoe and large antler implements, double-pointed pin, turkey metatarsal awl, disk shell beads, the circular gorget with a large central and two marginal holes. Many of these traits listed above are also found in the Spoon River Focus, such as the discoidal, double-pointed knife, triangular projectile points, expanding base drill, side-notched projectile points, antler-section hoe, turkey awl, and disk shell beads. The polished stone disk-shaped pipe which occurs in many Oneota sites is absent at Crable.

The Oneota type of vessels found at Crable is of the jar variety, which is typical for the Orr Focus. There is marked similarity between these types and those reported from other Oneota sites.

The pottery traits of the Grand River and Lake Winnebago foci have a somewhat wider differentiation from Crable than do those of the Orr Focus. The various traits used in the construction and decoration of the vessel constitute the main difference. The Lake Winnebago Focus pottery is like the Crable Oneota ware in its basic traits. The surface decorations are essentially like those found on the Crable and Orr Focus wares. In some of the brachiating designs there seems to be a high degree of similarity. The rims of the Lake Winnebago ware show many types of scalloping, and exhibit a greater variety of decorative techniques than do those found at Crable. The Lake Winnebago lip pie-crust crimping is not found at Crable but occurs on Orr Focus rims. Also, in the Lake Winnebago pottery there is a greater variety of rim types, with the degree of flare ranging from slight to pronounced, some being close to vertical, others horizontal.

[47] J. B. Griffin, 1943, p. 301.

[48] Ibid.

[49] The slate pendant at Crable may belong to the Maples Mills occupation of the area, as it was found by McGirr, who did not keep excavation notes.

The Grand River Focus pottery is different in some respects from the Orr and Lake Winnebago foci types and also from the Crable ware. The general type of surface decoration of Grand River Focus pottery is like that of Crable, but is mostly rough incised with little trailing. The use of three laterally directed, parallel, zigzag lines that encompass the shoulders of the vessels is common.[50] Although this design is not common at Crable it does occur, generally accompanied by punctates (Pl. VIII a). Occasionally notched or scalloped rims occur in the Grand River ware, which are like those found on the Lake Winnebago vessels. On the vertical rims of some of the Grand River vessels two holes appear across from each other, whose function may have been for suspension. This feature was not found at Crable.

The Orr Focus pottery varies to a certain extent from that at Crable (here only the jar forms with typical Oneota decorations will be compared). There is more leaching in the Orr Focus ware in Wisconsin, with the result that a large percentage of the vessels are softer. In many examples Crable vessels tend to have thicker walls than those of the Orr Focus. The Orr Focus sherds, because of their thinness, have a tendency to be cameoed on the interior when they are externally decorated. The funerary vessels of the Orr Focus are relatively rough and not as well executed as those used for utilitarian purposes. At Crable the funerary vessels are as well made as other vessels. In the shape of the body and the rims there is much similarity between the Orr and Crable materials. In decoration, too, the Orr Focus and Crable have much in common. Although cameoing occurs in the Orr Focus vessels, the narrow, rough incising which leaves no parallel cameo on the inner surface is far more prevalent.[51]

Designs typical of the Oneota type of decorations are found at Crable on other vessels besides the jar. The Crable and Orr Focus jars differ from those of Fort Ancient, although both areas have many traits in common. The decorative technique of both areas, to some extent similar, has distinctive variations such as the curvilinear guilloche and the effigy handles of Fort Ancient, while the jars themselves are not as squat as the Crable jars, and the overhanging collar found on the Fort Ancient vessel

[50] McKern, 1945, p. 149.
[51] Ibid., p. 147.

is not present at Crable. A Crable Deep Rimmed Plate sherd is reported by Griffin[52] as occurring in the Madisonville Focus, which indicates that there was some connection between these two groups.

In viewing Fort Ancient's relationship to Crable one sees that, though they differ in many respects, there was a mutual influence at work on these two groups and that there was some contact. It appears that they may be closely related in time, since white trade materials, although not common or abundant, appear only in the Madisonville Focus of the Fort Ancient Aspect. At Crable no trade materials have been found, but the close similarity between the Oneota materials of Crable and the Orr Focus of Iowa, where white trade materials are definitely found in association, shows that Crable comes very close to being fully historic.

The culture complex of Crable, for the most part, correlates quite closely with that of the Orr Focus. The traits found in the Orr Focus which are absent at Crable are the following: sheet copper pendants, disk pipes, inside cameos on the vessel resulting from outside decorative intaglios, a preponderance of notched and scalloped vessel lips, a simple variety of vessel shapes, and cannibalism. In viewing the whole complex of traits at Crable it is evident that the shell and bone complexes have more of a variety than those found in the Orr Focus. Ear spools, discoidals, sharpening stones, spades, and a variety of vessel shapes and ware types also occur. The variety of the shapes and the ware types at Crable is for the most part due to the presence of the Spoon River element.

In Jo Daviess County, Illinois, there appears what seems to be an early Upper Mississippi influence or development. Bennett is inclined to believe that "Upper Mississippi developed earlier than heretofore believed, and was contemporaneous with Middle Mississippi during a great portion of the history of the latter phase."[53] Donald Wray, in his research on Mississippian pottery, stated that the Trappist sherds from Jo Daviess sites are of an earlier type than those found at Crable.[54]

The Savannah site, while adhering to some Middle Mississippi traits, has many elements characteristic of Upper

[52] J. B. Griffin, 1943, p. 142.
[53] Bennett, op. cit.
[54] Personal communication.

Mississippi, such as the Upper Mississippi type of decorations occurring on the shoulder of the vessels, inside cameos, and snub-nosed scrapers. At Savannah there was more of an Oneota "complex" than was found at the Mills or Chapman sites. The Mills site was predominantly Middle Mississippi with slight evidence of Oneota influence or development, while the Chapman site, closely affiliated with the Mills site, had no tangible evidence of the Southern Cult, and no historical materials were found.

In Fulton County, in general, the Middle Mississippi sites appear earlier than the Crable site, since few of the features characteristic of Upper Mississippi and the Southern Cult appear in them, although at Fv47, Fv49, and Fo19 Oneota-like elements occur on some sherds, suggesting some weak Upper Mississippi influences. These Oneota elements are of the Crable type and not of the Jo Daviess earlier "transition" type. At Kingston Lake the bone beamer was found, an artifact that appears in Upper Mississippi sites, such as the Huber and Fisher sites in northeastern Illinois, the Grand River Focus sites in Wisconsin, and the Fort Ancient Aspect sites in Ohio, and in some Hopewell sites. At Kingston Lake a few Crable Trailed sherds are present.[55] Donald Wray also stated that at the Kingston Lake site a Southern Cult-like design appears on a beaker. This is not conclusive evidence that the Southern Cult existed there but hints of late influence. Thus, it appears in Fulton County that Crable was inhabited after the surrounding sites in the immediate vicinity has been abandoned or were dying out. This must be assumed since few traits other than those of the Middle Mississippi Phase are found in any of the surrounding Mississippi and Middle Mississippi sites. As traits of these two taxonomic groups are sometimes combined on one type of specimen from the bottom stratum to the top, it is evident that they formed a fused cultural whole during the habitation of Crable.

The Huber Component differs from the Crable Upper Mississippi material by the use of the "pie-crust" rim and the employment of "finger-grooves" on the shoulder that left a cameo impression on the interior. The bone beamer was also found, as has been mentioned. On the whole, Huber, like Crable, is

[55] Information from files in Ceramic Repository, Museum of Anthropology, University of Michigan.

close to the Orr Focus materials: Huber is Oneota; Crable is predominantly Spoon River.

In the Milan Mound Group, Rock Island County, Illinois, Oneota pottery similar to that from Crable is found in association with Middle Mississippi vessels; this is also true of vessels that came from Eliza Township in Mercer County, Illinois.[56] These sites are closer to the Orr Focus "homeland" and therefore would be expected to show such associations. It appears that from the Crable site westward to the Orr Focus sites of Iowa there is an area where the late Middle Mississippi sites are mixed with Oneota.

The Fisher Focus has many traits in common with both the Fort Ancient Aspect and Oneota; however, there are certain characteristics that separate the Fisher Focus from both of these.[57] The pottery from the Fisher site has closer affiliations with the Oneota type than with the Fort Ancient. In vessel shape, rim shape, placement of decoration on the shoulder area, the decorating of the handle, and in the style of decoration Fisher vessels have similarities to the Crable jars. Fisher jars differ from those of Crable in that the vessels were cordmarked before the trailed decoration was applied. The trailing itself was deeply impressed on the thin ware, leaving cameos on the inside surface. These designs appear on grit-tempered and shell-tempered vessels; on both types of vessels "finger grooves" or nodes sometimes appear.

When the evidence of Upper Mississippi in the Illinois and Iowa area is viewed, a time difference as well as local variations is discerned. The Upper Mississippi elements in the Jo Daviess sites are seen by Bennett to be "immediately antecedent to Oneota Upper Mississippi, and it would be impossible to account for the resemblances on the basis of 'influence' from Oneota."[58] He has accepted the idea that the Mills, Chapman, and Savannah sites were a phase in the Middle Mississippi cultural development when it began to differentiate into a western Upper Mississippi tradition. The Jo Daviess material appears older than Crable, as the Southern Cult elements are absent and Old Village characteristics are more abundant.

[56] Information from files in Ceramic Repository, Museum of Anthropology, University of Michigan.

[57] For a summary of the Fisher Focus see J. B. Griffin, 1943, pp. 283-84.

[58] *Op. cit.*, p. 157.

At Crable the association of the Trappist-Spoon River materials with those of Oneota suggests that the former manifestation continued into relatively late, if not historic, times. To date no white trade materials have been found in association with the Fulton County Middle Mississippi sites except the one possibly historic Middle Mississippi site reported by Powell.[59] The general Spoon River sites may be placed in an earlier period, since few of the features characteristic of the historic Orr Focus complex are present except at Crable and at a few other sites mentioned in this connection, where only a few sherds carrying the Oneota decorative style occur. The Oneota material present at Crable is not like that mentioned by Bennett for Jo Daviess County, but it is a fully developed Oneota style.

In the northern part of Illinois besides Fisher and Huber sites are those of Plum Island,[60] Starved Rock State Park,[61] Gentleman Farm,[62] and Forest Home.[63] The southernmost Oneota site is Pere Marquette,[64] which is located near the juncture of the Illinois and the Mississippi rivers. Of these sites Plum Island, Gentleman Farm, Huber, and Pere Marquette, like Crable, did not have associated historic materials. Because of this fact one would place these sites earlier than 1673. Also these sites, like Crable, do not represent a stage of developmental Upper Mississippi, since the Oneota elements found at Crable, Pere Marquette, and Huber are fully developed. The Fisher type of Upper Mississippi occurring at Plum Island is also well developed.

On the north side of the Illinois River across from Starved Rock, the University of Chicago excavated the Zimmerman site[65] during the summer of 1947. Prior to this time Donald Wray and I had made surface collections from this site, and Richard MacNeish[66] had tested the area. In association with white trade

[59] Op. cit.

[60] Kelly and Cole, 1931, pp. 320-26.

[61] Morgan, 1948, pp. 274-75, and personal communication with Thomas Lee.

[62] Molly Allee, personal communication.

[63] Morgan, 1932.

[64] Rinaldo, 1937.

[65] Morgan, 1948, and personal communication with William Sears and Thomas Lee.

[66] Personal communication.

materials were found Fisher, Fort Ancient, Oneota, and Late Woodland sherds. A similar type of site without trade materials is located on the St. Joseph River, one mile north of Buchanan, Michigan.[67] This was excavated by the Museum of Anthropology, of the University of Michigan. Here, however, the Oneota influence is not as strong as at the Zimmerman site, but Fisher types such as Langford Trailed and Langford Corded[68] were numerous.

During the summer of 1948 the University of Chicago excavated the area on top of Starved Rock and in the late sections of the site found materials comparable to those from the Zimmerman site, across the river. One exception is noted: no Oneota sherds were present.[69] The Fisher element was present in large amounts and may have crowded out the Oneota element. Since there is historical reference to the location of a number of differing ethnic groups in the area during this time period, one would expect various cultural types to be present. One sees, however, that the Oneota was in the area, being contemporaneous with Fisher during a certain part of the time, and that at a later date the Oneota died out, giving way to Fisher.

The Gentleman Farm, which has Fisher materials, falls into the middle phase (Phase B and possibly early Phase C[70]) of the Upper Mississippi occupation at the Fisher site. This site was, I believe, in existence at the same time as Huber, Plum Island, Pere Marquette, and Crable.

John Griffin,[71] in his work on the Fisher site, noted that throughout the Upper Mississippi occupation at Fisher there was contact with Middle Mississippi. He believed that there was contemporaneity with the Spoon River Focus. Throughout a period of time, from the inception of Upper Mississippi at Fisher there was a shift to a Woodland-like culture and away from an Upper Mississippi with Middle Mississippi contacts. The nature of the development of Fisher then was different from that which occurred at the Crable site in which Oneota, fully developed, has very strong Middle Mississippi elements. John Griffin sees the early Upper Mississippi "as Upper Mississippi formed by Middle Mississippi

[67] Excavated during the summer of 1948.
[68] J. W. Griffin, 1948.
[69] Personal communication with Thomas Lee.
[70] J. W. Griffin, 1946.
[71] J. W. Griffin, 1946, 1948.

distribution."[72] At Crable, assuming that the Oneota evolved in the Iowa-Wisconsin-Minnesota area, one sees that it was well developed during the close of the Middle Mississippi times in the north, while Middle Mississippi was still strong in the Spoon River "homeland." As noted at Fisher, this shift from a Middle Mississippi culture to that of a blended or interrelated cultural whole was not a sharp break, but a "peaceful" amalgamation and development.

POSSIBLE ETHNIC CONNECTIONS OF CRABLE

Since the Upper Mississippi influence is present at Crable and has a high degree of correlation with the occurrence of the traits at Oneota sites in Iowa as described by Mott,[73] Keyes,[74] and McKern,[75] a hypothetical statement might be made as to the identity of the peoples who lived at Crable. James B. Griffin[76] has tentatively suggested that the Oneota Aspect is traceable to the Chiwere Sioux Indians. According to Mott: "Tradition states that the Ioway originally came into the area now Iowa from the east."[77] It is therefore possible that the Crable site yields remains of the Ioway Indians or of a group closely related in culture, as there is a close relationship archaeologically between the two areas.

Also historically there was much contact between the groups in these two areas. Mott[78] has tentatively identified the Orr Focus in Iowa with the Ioway Indians, but, as has already been noted, it is doubtful whether Crable belongs to the Orr Focus. The logical conclusion, therefore, is that some other aboriginal group, aside from the Ioway but closely related, may have been responsible for Crable.

The Peoria Indians were in the Fulton County area at the time

[72] J. W. Griffin, 1948.
[73] Mott, 1938, pp. 227-327.
[74] Keyes, 1927.
[75] McKern, 1945.
[76] J. B. Griffin, 1937, p. 180.
[77] Mott, 1938, p. 304.
[78] *Ibid.*

of the first white contact, Marquette's voyage down the Mississippi in 1673-1674. The Peoria Indians belonged to the Illinois Confederacy, whose principal groups were the Cahokia, Kaskaskia, Michigamea, Moingwena, Peoria, and Tamaroa. In a group of selected maps published by S. J. Tucker[79] one sees that the only group noted in the Lake Peoria area is the Peoria tribe.

Before evaluating the evidence for the possible identification of the ethnic group responsible for the Crable materials, one should examine what has been done with the Oneota in areas outside of Illinois. The distribution of Oneota in Iowa is extensive, with the sites occurring along various watercourses. In the eastern part of the state they occur along the Upper Iowa River, in Winneshiek and Allamakee counties, and in the southeastern part sites are located along the Mississippi River in Muscatine, Louisa, and Des Moines counties, while the western sites are located around Spiri and Okaboji lakes and on the Little Sioux River in Clay, Dickinson, and Woodbury counties. The most westerly sites are in Lyon County on the Big Sioux River.

The presence of materials, such as brass ear coils, glass beads, and iron objects is definite proof that this culture was in existence when European objects were being freely traded among the Indians, and that it is later than the other cultural horizons in the area.

The first documented white contact or entry into this region was in 1673 for tribes on the Mississippi and was some years later for the groups in the interior of the state. The Ioway, a group of the Chiwere Sioux, as has been noted, were present when this contact was made. European influence had not yet caused a degeneration of their material culture. Other groups of the Chiwere Sioux were the Oto and Missouri. These were close culturally and linguistically to the Winnebago. It is believed that the Oto were responsible for the Oneota in the northwestern part of Iowa.

Other groups which were in this area for only a short time were the Kickapoo, Illinois, Sauk, Fox, Omaha, and Miami. The Kickapoo lived at the mouth of the Upper Iowa for a few years but as a group did not penetrate far into the territory of the Ioway. The Illinois and the Miami had contact with the Ioway on the Des Moines River (or Iowa River) in the southeastern part of the state from 1650 to about 1676. It has been noted

[79] Tucker, 1942.

that the Mocassin Bluff site has Oneota elements mixed with the late Woodland and Fisher materials. This site probably belonged to a Miami group in the area in protohistoric (if not early historic) times.[80] The Sauk and the Fox were also in the southeastern part of the state but did not go much farther west. Since all of these above-mentioned groups arrived late and remained for only a short time, the opportunity for them to leave much evidence of extensive occupation is slight. Enough evidence is present, however, to show that contacts were made in the historic and protohistoric times, which may or may not have taken place in prehistoric times.

In Wisconsin the distribution of the Oneota, as it is now known, is centered in the lower half of the state, extending southwestward from the shores of Green Bay to Lake Winnebago and on to the Mississippi River, probably via the lower Wisconsin River. On the western shores of Lake Winnebago, Oneota occurs as an island surrounded by a Woodland culture. These Oneota sites are known as historic Winnebago of the early historic period.[81] The tribes occupying these sites retained their culture, which was shared by some other Siouan groups, such as the Ioway, despite close contacts with the peoples of another culture. These close contacts with Woodland peoples, or isolation from Siouan peoples in the Lake Winnebago region, had an effect on the culture of the group along the western shores of the lake and on the group in Green Lake County, both of which have a local development and have been placed in separate foci from the other Oneota sites to the west. These foci are Lake Winnebago and Grand River. The southwestern Wisconsin sites have been associated with the Orr Focus and with the Ioway Indians.

In historic times the Winnebago were surrounded by Central Algonkin peoples, such as the Menominee, Fox, and Sauk, who were probably the descendants of the protohistoric Woodland groups in the area.

In Minnesota the Oneota sites which have so far been investigated are in the southern sixth of the state, located in the counties of Huston, Fillmore, Nicollet, Faribault, and Blue Earth. The Orr Focus has its distribution in the southeastern

[80] J. B. Griffin, personal communication.

[81] There is some doubt as to which river Marquette had reference; see Mott, 1938, and Delanglez 1946-49.

part of the state, but it differs somewhat from the Iowa Oneota. The Orr Focus, for example, has rock-capped mounds. In the south central part of Minnesota the Blue Earth Focus occurs, which has not yet been identified with any ethnological group. The Cambria culture, whose type site is on the Upper Minnesota River near Cambria, Minnesota, has some traits of each of three phases: the Upper, Middle, and Plains Mississippi phases, but it cannot be definitely classified as belonging to any one of them.[82]

Oneota pottery, as trade ware, has been found at Big Stone Lake, which is on the state line separating Minnesota and South Dakota, and near Leech Lake in the north central part of the state.[83]

The evidence in South Dakota is very meager. An Oneota site was located at the mouth of the Vermillion River at its juncture with the Missouri; this site is identified with the Ioway site on Delisle's 1718 map.[84] In Stanley County, on the Missouri River, there is evidence of Oneota occupation,[85] but no definitive publication has been made, and its exact relationship to the rest of the area is unknown.

The Leary site[86] in Richardson County, Nebraska, is a precontact Oneota site, which is believed to belong to the Oto.[87] An earth lodge was found that, according to Griffin,[88] resembles the surface Middle Mississippi house type rather than that of Fisher in Illinois, which is not an earth lodge. On the Elkhorn River at Stanton, Nebraska, circular house pits were found associated with the Oneota Aspect. This site is said to belong to the contact period, as copper kettles and old American bottles were found.[89]

Near Lynch, Holt County, Nebraska, circular house pits with entranceways to the east and southeast occur, which are related to the Upper Mississippi Phase. The artifacts and pottery

[82] Wilford, 1945, p. 39.
[83] Wilford, 1941.
[84] Mott, 1938, p. 302.
[85] McKern, 1945, p. 168.
[86] Hill and Wedel, 1936.
[87] Mott, 1938, p. 258.
[88] J. W. Griffin, 1944.
[89] Bell, 1939, but the evidence supporting this association has not yet appeared.

are identical with the historic Ponca materials in Knox County, even to the use of crushed bone for tempering.[90] Bell[91] found no evidence that the Ponca ever came into contact or conflict with the rectangular-house peoples who possess the Upper Republican and Nebraska cultures. The Ponca may belong to the Oneota Aspect, since they have no relationship to the Upper Republican and Nebraska cultures and since no other aspect of Upper Mississippi is apparent in the region. The Ponca were a Dhegiha Siouan group, of which the Omaha, Osage, and Kansa were also members. The Osage are now considered Oneota by archaeologists in Missouri.[92]

The westward extension of the Oneota is along the Loup River, where it is partially contemporary with the protohistoric Pawnee, as is shown by mutual cross finds of sherds and other items.[93]

In viewing some of the cultural influences which took part in the last major stage of Nebraskan prehistory, one finds that the Oneota were coming through Iowa and Missouri; Middle Mississippi of the Cahokia type was moving through Missouri and out onto the Plains, while in Nebraska the Upper Republican cultures were already deeply rooted, having their affiliations to the east and southeast. Because of the complexity of the problem in protohistoric and historic times the picture is not as easy to view as it might have been if the cultural changes had not been so rapid. These rapid changes were due to the movements of various peoples under European pressure. The Oneota Aspect in Nebraska has been correlated with the Oto; it is an extension of the Oto in Iowa.

Oneota sites have been reported from Brown and Republican counties, in the northern part of Kansas, but as yet have not been correlated with a historical group, although the temptation is great to equate them with the Kansa or the Osage. From their position they could have been Oneota, or they may have received influences either from Oneota peoples coming up the Missouri River or from peoples moving overland from the Iowa-Nebraska area.

In Missouri some of the Oneota sites are so located in time

[90] Ibid.
[91] Ibid.
[92] Berry, Chapman, and Mack, 1944.
[93] Wedel, 1940, p. 336.

and space that Berry and Chapman[94] have attributed this horizon to the Missouri and possibly to the Osage,[95] the Missouri being Chiwere Sioux and the Osage, Dhegiha Sioux. These sites occur in Saline, Howard, Bates, and Vernon counties. The Chiwere Oneota sites occur on the Missouri River, and the Dhegiha Oneota on the Little Osage and its tributaries. This area is equally distant from known sites in Illinois, Iowa, and Nebraska but seems to show closer affiliations with Nebraska than with the other areas. This seems logical, as one would think that the influences or peoples moved up and down the Missouri River near which the Oneota sites are located in both regions.

In a summary of this western section of the Oneota, one sees that the Oneota had some contacts with other groups which carried a different culture, such as Algonkin, Woodland, and Middle Mississippi. The Oneota Aspect has been equated with various historic Siouan groups which in turn had associations with non-Siouan groups. The Chiwere Sioux have been identified with the Winnebago of Wisconsin, with the Ioway of Iowa, Minnesota, Wisconsin, and South Dakota, with the Oto of Iowa and Nebraska, and with the Missouri in Missouri. Of the Dhegiha Siouan group it is highly probable that the Osage of Missouri and possibly the Ponca of Nebraska will be more definitely correlated with the Oneota Aspect.[95a]

In Illinois at the time of the explorations of Marquette and Joliet the Illinois Indians were the only permanent residents of the area from the Rock River south to the Ohio River and west to the Mississippi. The Peoria group was definitely established in the Spoon River area and extended west to the Mississippi.[96]

It should be noted that the area occupied by the Illinois at the time of historic contact coincides closely with the distribution of Middle and Upper Mississippi manifestations in Illinois. In the Fulton County area one sees that there is no sharp break between the Spoon River Aspect and the advent of the Oneota; this is exemplified by the material from Crable and from other sites in the area having Oneota sherds. Since there is no sharp break in the cultural continuum and since the Peoria were well established in the area, it is logical to suggest that the Peoria were responsible for the material culture found at Crable.[97]

[94] Berry and Chapman, 1942.

[95] Berry, Chapman, and Mack, 1944.

[95a] This association is viewed with considerable skepticism by the editor of this series.

[96] Hodge, 1907-1910, p. 228.

[97] Wray and Smith, 1943, 1944.

As has been seen, Oneota has not been equated with an Algonkin group in any other area, but this does not necessitate the conclusion that it must always be Siouan wherever it is found.

One sees that the Illinois had historical contacts with many groups to their north and west. The first mention of the Illinois is in the Jesuit Relation for 1660,[98] which tells about this group then living to the west of Green Bay, Wisconsin. Besides mentioning villages of Illinois it also states the fact that groups from the Illinois River were making regular trips by 1667 to La Pointe on Lake Superior to trade furs.[99] At this period the group is believed to have extended into southern Wisconsin, northern Illinois, and sections of Iowa and Missouri.[100] It is a little difficult to place the Illinois exactly during this time, as they had been under pressure from the Iroquois since 1655 and had moved out of their homeland. The group was driven from the Illinois area as the Iroquois eventually pressed on to the Mississippi River. The raids of the Iroquois lasted until 1680.[101] During this time the Illinois were in a position to be in close contact with the Ioway, or the carriers of the Oneota culture. Marquette on his voyage encountered the Peoria Indians on the west bank of the Mississippi River, near the mouth of the Des Moines River (Iowa River).[102] The next year on the return trip up the Illinois, he found the same group or a related group of the Peoria established near the south end of Lake Peoria. Joliet in 1674 showed two villages of Illinois on the Des Moines River (Iowa River) near villages of Ponca and Omaha. Also at this time the Kaskaskia were located near Utica, Illinois.[103] Franquelin[104] in 1684 also placed the village of the Kaskaskia at Utica and showed that it was within a few miles of various Miami villages. On this map the village of the Peoria at Lake Peoria is not shown but instead Fort Creve Coeur is indicated.[105] This fort was established by Tonti, and it is known that the Peoria village

[98] Margry, 1878-1886, vol. 1.

[99] Hodge, 1907-1910, pp. 228, 598.

[100] Ibid.

[101] For a review of the Illinois-Iroquois wars see Hunt, 1940, whose discussion is well documented.

[102] Marquette, 1853, p. 244.

[103] Joliet map.

[104] Map from Tucker.

[105] This site is close to the site reported by Powell, op. cit.

did exist at the fort. By 1688 the Illinois were consolidating themselves in a smaller area, as were the Kickapoo on the Rock River and the Mascouten on the upper Fox River.[106]

This southern migration of northern groups went on until late in the eighteenth century. For a time the Illinois village at Kaskaskia remained in the Starved Rock area. In 1694 the Kaskaskia abandoned their village near Utica and joined the Peoria, and in 1700 went to the site on the Mississippi, below St. Louis, which bears their name.[107]

The Illinois made frequent raids on the Pawnee in order to obtain slaves.[108] On Le Seuer's map of 1701[109] some of the Pawnee groups were shown directly west of the Peoria, who were west of the Missouri River. In order to obtain these people as slaves, the Illinois parties traveled through the Oneota territory, which probably is indicative of a friendly relationship between these two groups. Thus, for a number of years the Illinois had contacts farther west, some of them lasting over an extended period of time.[110]

Mississippi sites in the Fulton County area (in which Oneota cultural concepts appear) can be attributed only to the Illinois Indians, since they were the only ethnic group in the area. These sites cannot be attributed to the Fox, Sauk, and Pottawatomie, since they came into the area after 1725; nor can they be attributed to the Winnebago, who had many white trade items when they moved southward in historic times to the Rock River.

The work done by the University of Chicago at the Zimmerman site revealed a majority of Fisher and Oneota sherds, associated with white trade materials. Since this site dates from about 1665 to 1720 plus or minus, the Upper Mississippi culture in the Starved Rock areas was probably carried on during this time by the Illinois, who were the dominant group in the area.

Relationships also existed between the Illinois and the Shawnee

[106] Franquelin map from Tucker.
[107] Gravier, 1900.
[108] Kinietz, 1940, from Raudot Letter, 1710.
[109] Wedel, 1936, map 4.
[110] In dealing with this problem circumstantial evidence has been used in interpreting one of the more likely causes of events and the cultural processes involved.

as Griffin[111] has pointed out. It has been suggested[112] by Kenneth Orr that the Fort Ancient unit at the Zimmerman site may represent the visiting Shawnee.

It is interesting to note that in the Madisonville Focus[113] a Crable Deep Rimmed Plate-like sherd was found.

In Fulton County at an earlier time, the Peoria were in a position to take over the Middle Mississippi culture that pushed up the Illinois and Mississippi River valleys. At Crable these southern influences were still being felt, as is noted by the presence of pottery types from the southeastern Missouri and northwestern Arkansas areas. The Peoria also by the nature of their position were in the critical place, in both time and space, to receive influence from the Oneota culture of Missouri, Iowa, and Wisconsin.

[111] J. B. Griffin, 1943, pp. 24-25.
[112] Morgan, 1948.
[113] J. B. Griffin, op. cit.

SELECTED BIBLIOGRAPHY

Adams, Robert McCormick

1941 Archaeological Investigations in Jefferson County, Missouri, 1939-40. Trans. Acad. Sci. St. Louis, 30, No. 4: 151-221.

Bell, E. H.

1939 Great Plains Area. Amer. Antiq., IV, No. 4: 355-57.

Bennett, John

1945 Archaeological Explorations in Jo Daviess County, Illinois. Chicago: Univ. Chicago Press.

Berry, B., C. Chapman, and J. Mack

1944 Archaeological Remains of the Osage. Amer. Antiq., X, No. 1: 1-11.

Berry, B., and C. Chapman

1942 An Oneota Site in Missouri. Amer. Antiq., VII, No. 3: 290-305.

Cole, Fay-Cooper, and Thorne Deuel

1937 Rediscovering Illinois; Archaeological Explorations in and Around Fulton County. Chicago: Univ. Chicago Press.

Delanglez, Jean

1946-49 (Various articles) Mid-America, An Historical Review. N.S. Vols. 17-18, 19-20.

Gravier, Jacques

1900 Relation. The Jesuit Relations and Allied Documents. Ed. by R. G. Thwaites. Cleveland: Burrows Brothers. LXIV: 158ff.; LXV: 100-103.

Griffin, James B.

1937 The Archaeological Remains of the Chiwere Sioux. Amer. Antiq., II, No. 3: 180-81.

1943 The Fort Ancient Aspect, Its Cultural and Chronological Position in Mississippi Valley Archaeology. Ann Arbor: Univ. Mich. Press.

1949 The Cahokia Ceramic Complexes. Proc. Fifth Plains Conf. Archeol., Lab. Anthropol. Univ. Neb., Notebook 1: 44-58.

Griffin, James B., and Richard G. Morgan, editors

1941 Contributions to the Archaeology of the Illinois River Valley. Trans. Amer. Phil. Soc., n.s., XXXII, Pt. 1.

Griffin, John W.

1944 New Evidence from the Fisher Site. Ill. Acad. Sci. Trans., 37: 37-40.

1946 The Upper Mississippi Occupations of the Fisher Site. Master's thesis, University of Chicago.

1948 Upper Mississippi at the Fisher Site. Amer. Antiq., XIV, No. 2: 124-26.

Harrington, M. R.
1920 Certain Caddo Sites in Arkansas. Mus. Amer. Indian, Heye Found. Indian Notes and Monogr., Misc. Papers, No. 10.

Hill, A. T., and Waldo Wedel
1936 Excavations at the Leary Indian Village and Burial Site, Richardson County, Nebraska. Neb. Hist. Mag., XVII, No. 1: 2-73.

Hodge, Frederick W., editor
1907-1910 Handbook of the American Indians North of Mexico. Bur. Amer. Ethnol. Bull., No. 30. 2 vols.

Hunt, George T.
1940 The Wars of the Iroquois, A Study in Intertribal Trade Relations. Madison: Univ. Wisconsin Press.

Kelly, Arthur R., and Fay-Cooper Cole
1931 Rediscovering Illinois. In: Blue Book of the State of Illinois, 1931-1932. Springfield: State of Illinois. Pp. 318-41.

Keyes, Charles R.
1927 Prehistoric Man in Iowa. Palimpsest, VIII, No. 6: 185-229.

Kinietz, W. Vernon
1940 The Indians of the Western Great Lakes, 1615-1760. Occ. Contrib. Mus. Anthropol. Univ. Mich., No. 10.

McKern, W. C.
1931 Wisconsin Pottery. Amer. Anthropol., 33, No. 3: 383-89.
1945 Preliminary Report on the Upper Mississippi Phase in Wisconsin. Bull. Public Mus. City of Milwaukee, 16, No. 3.

Margry, Pierre
1878-86 Mémoires et documents pour servir a l'histoire des origines françaises de pays d'outre-mer: découvertes et établissements des français dans le sud d'Amérique septentrionale, 1615-1754. Paris: D. Jouaust. 6 vols.

Marquette, Jacques
1853 Récit des voyages et des découvertes. In: Discovery and Exploration of the Mississippi Valley, by John Gilmary Shea. New York: J. S. Redfield.

Moore, C. B.
1910 Antiquities of the St. Francis, White, and Black Rivers, Arkansas. Journ. Acad. Nat. Sci. Phila., 2d. Ser., XIV, Pt. 2.

Morgan, Richard G.
1932 Archaeology of the Chicago Area. Trans. Ill. State Acad. Sci., XXV, No. 4: 91-93.

1948 Northern Mississippi Valley. Amer. Antiq., XIII, No. 3: 274-75.

Mott, Mildred
1938 The Relation of Historic Indian Tribes to Archaeological Manifestations in Iowa. Iowa Journ. Hist. and Pol., XXXVI, No. 3: 227-337.

Neumann, Georg K.
1940 Evidence for the Antiquity of Scalping from Central Illinois. Amer. Antiq., V, No. 4: 287-89.

Phillips, Philip, James A. Ford, and James B. Griffin
n.d. Archaeological Survey in the Lower Mississippi Alluvial Valley, 1940-1947. Papers Peabody Mus. Archaeol. and Ethnol., 25. (In press.)

Powell, J. W.
1894 Administrative Report. 12th Annual Report, Bur. Amer. Ethnol. pp. xxxix-xl.

Rinaldo, J. B.
1937 MS, The Pere Marquette Park Sites. Master's thesis, Universit of Chicago.

Root, T. B.
1938 Summarized Account of the Pleistocene Geology of the Lower Illinois River Valley. (Part of Ph.D. thesis, University of Chicago, 1935. Privately published.)

Simpson, A. M.
1936 Archaeological Survey of Peoria County. Trans. Illinois State Acad. Sci., XXIX.

Snyder, J. F.
1908 The Brown County Ossuary. Journ. Illinois State Hist. Soc., 1, Nos. 2-3: 33-43.

Strong, W. D.
1940 From History to Prehistory in the Northern Great Plains. In: Essays in Historical Anthropology of North America. Smithson. Misc. Coll., 100: 353-94.

Titterington, Paul F.
1938 The Cahokia Mound Group and Its Village Site Material. St. Louis: Published by the author.

Tucker, Sara Jones
1942 Indian Villages of the Illinois Country. Scientific Papers, Ill. State Mus., 2, Pt. 1.

Waring, Antonio, Jr., and Preston Holder
1945 A Prehistoric Ceremonial Complex in the Southeastern United States. Amer. Anthropol., 43, No. 1: 1-34.

Wedel, Waldo R.

1936 An Introduction to Pawnee Archaeology. Bur. Amer. Ethnol. Bull., No. 112.

1940 Cultural Sequences in the Central Great Plains. In: Essays in Historical Anthropology of North America. Smithson. Misc. Coll., 100: 291-352.

Wilford, L. A.

1941 A Tentative Classification of the Prehistoric Cultures of Minnesota. Amer. Antiq., VI, No. 3: 231-49.

1945 Three Village Sites of the Mississippi Pattern in Minnesota. Ibid., XI, No. 1: 32-40.

Wray, Donald, and Hale Smith

1943 The Illinois Confederacy and Middle Mississippian Culture in Illinois. Trans. Ill. Acad. Sci., 36, No. 2: 82-86.

1944 An Hypothesis for the Identification of the Illinois Confederacy with the Middle Mississippi Culture in Illinois. Amer. Antiq., X, No. 1: 23-27.

PLATE I

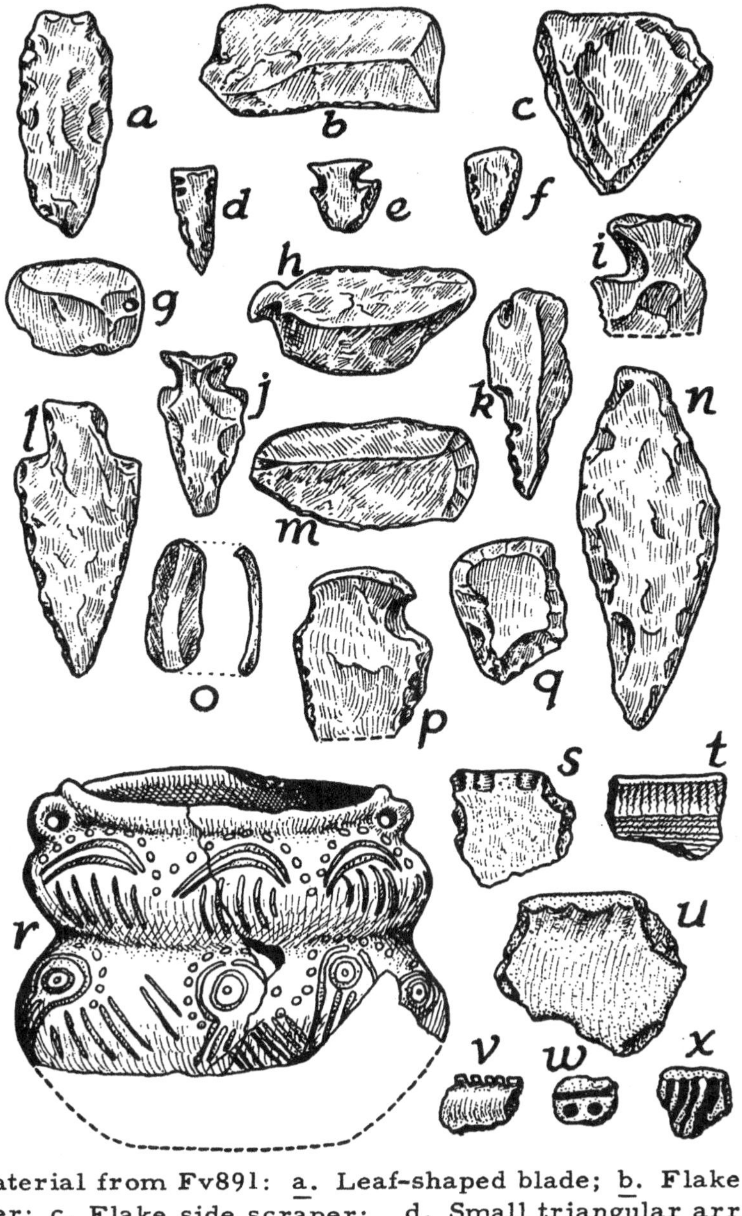

Material from Fv891: a. Leaf-shaped blade; b. Flake side scraper; c. Flake side scraper; d. Small triangular arrow point; e. Small corner-notched point; f. End scraper; g. Side scraper; h. Tang scraper; i. Basal half of corner-notched projectile point; j. Side-notched projectile point; k. Flake scraper; l. Stemmed projectile point; m. Scraper; n. Knife blade; o. Flake scraper; p. Basal half of projectile point; q. Scraper; r. Kerton Incised compound vessel, "weeping eye" motif; s-x. Maples Mills rim sherds.

PLATE II

a. View of the twenty-foot profile of Fo892 showing features II and III, burial pits.

b. Burials from Fc896, from front to rear of pictures are burials 5, 6, 7, 8, 9.

PLATE III

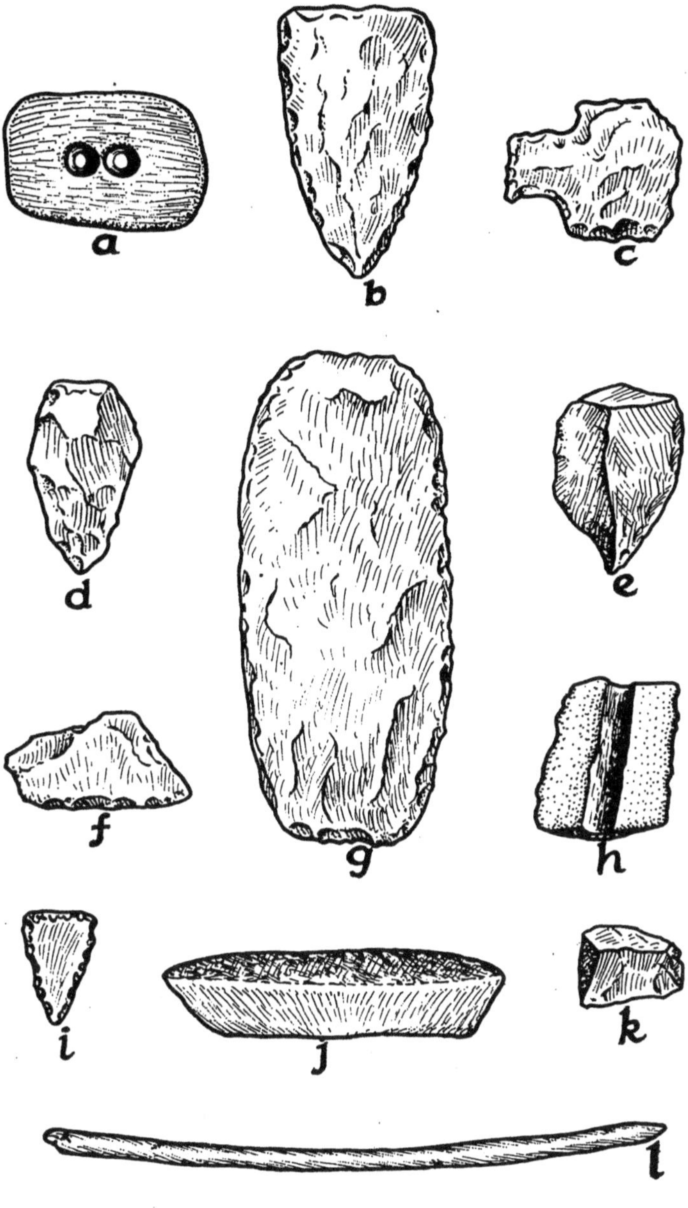

semblage of artifacts from Fo894: a. Shell gorget; b. Triangular
ojectile point; c. Base of stemmed projectile point; d. Leaf-shaped
ide; e. Graver; f. Flake scraper; g. Large flint implement, pos-
oly a hoe; h. Arrow-shaft smoother; i. Small triangular projectile
int; j. Bone scraper; k. Section of flake; l. Bone pin or needle.

PLATE IV

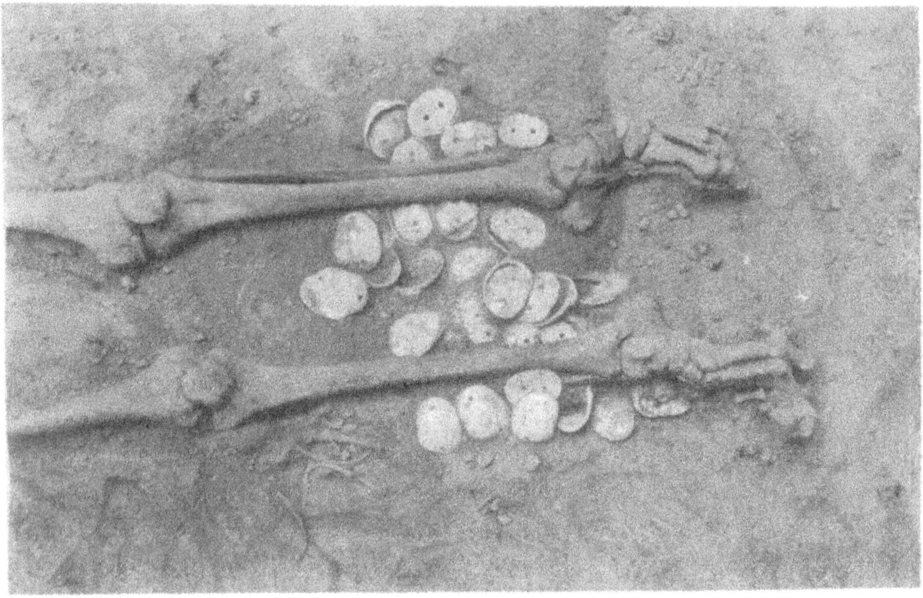

a. Shell rattles around ankles of burial Fc896-11.

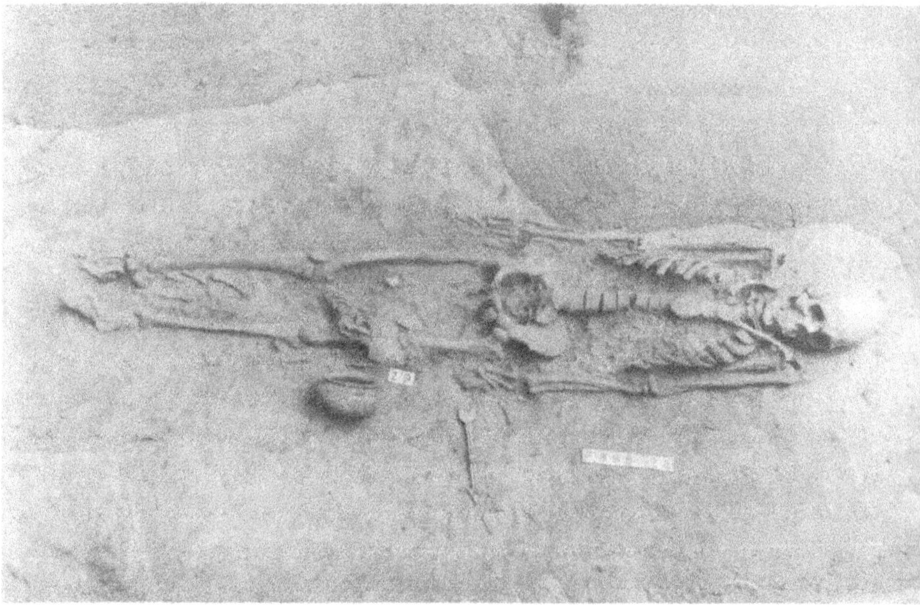

b. Burials Fc896-28 and 29.

PLATE V

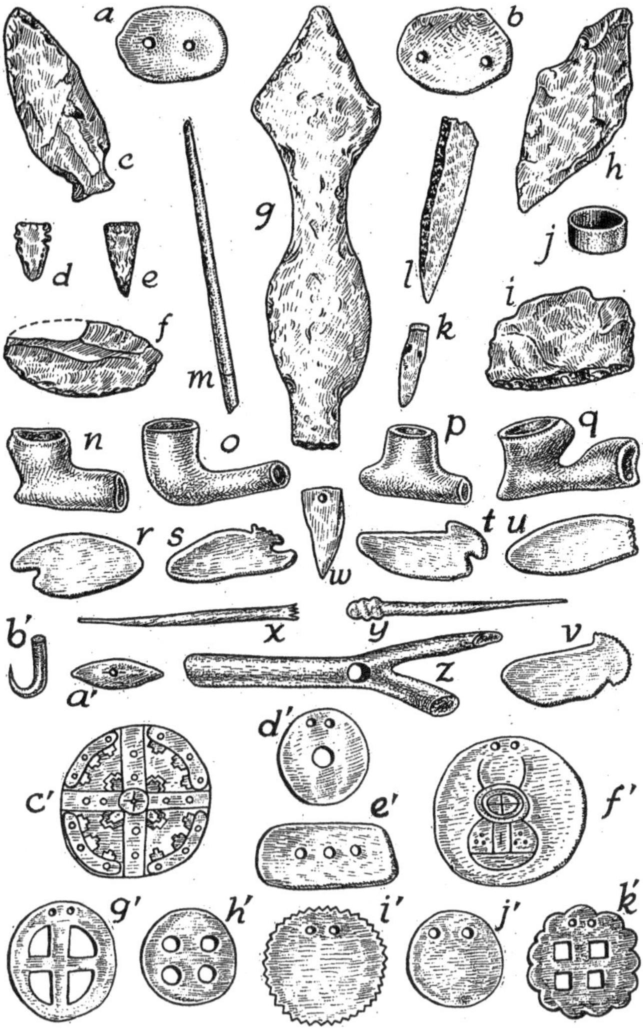

Materials in the McGirr Collection from Fo896: a-b. Top and bottom of a shell rattle; c. Projectile point; d. Multiple side-notched small triangular projectile point; e. Triangular projectile point; f. Ovoid side scraper; g. Broken flint mace; h. Grooved knife blade; i. Flint scraper; j. Bone ring; k. Drill; l. Narrow side scraper; m. Broken bone needle or awl; n,q. Clay equal-armed elbow pipes; o-p. Ground stone pipes; r-w. Shell spoons; x-y. Bone pins; z. Antler arrow-shaft straightener; a'. Perforated bone; b'. Unbarbed bone fishhook; c'-k'. Shell gorgets.

PLATE VI

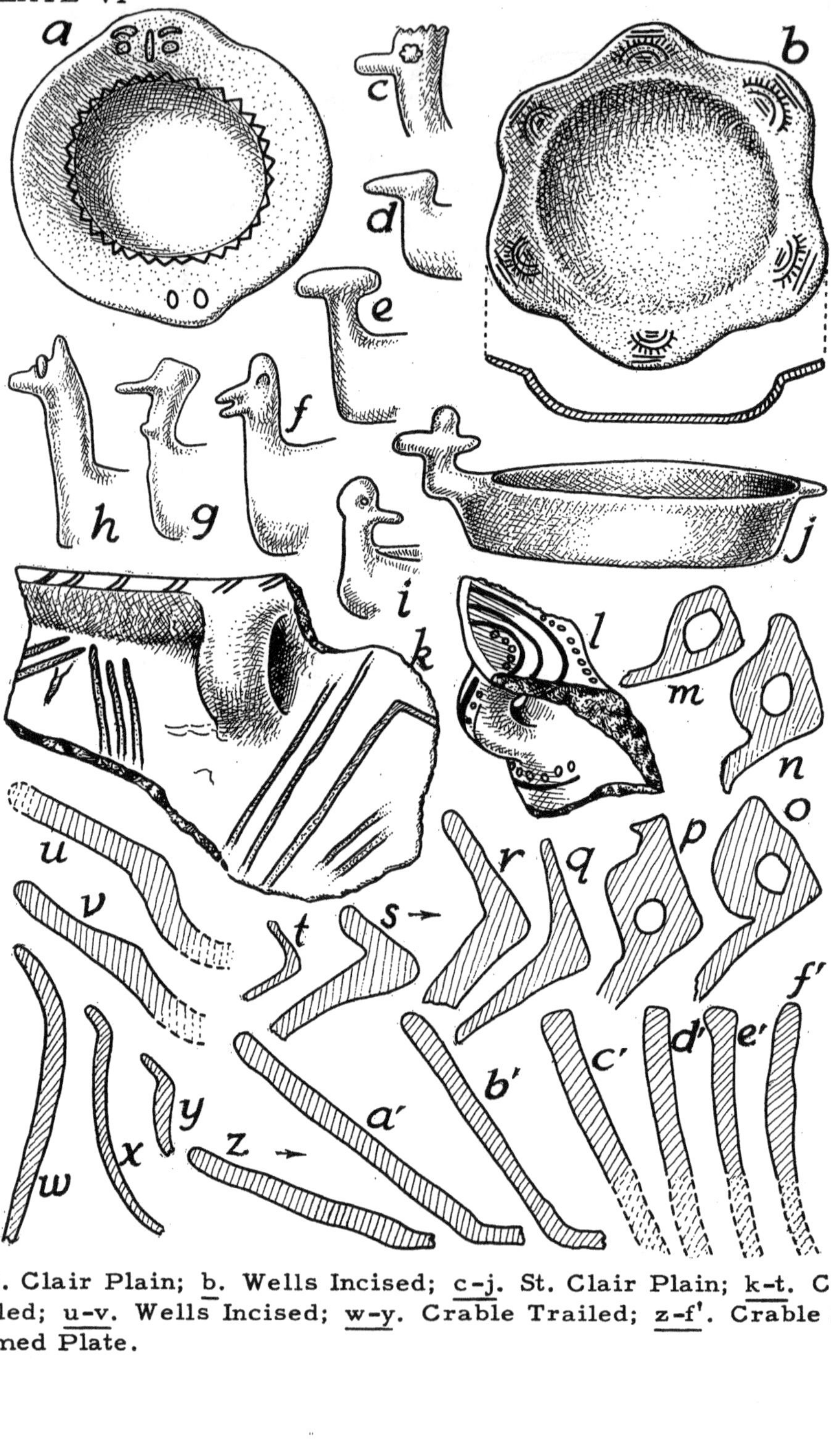

a. St. Clair Plain; b. Wells Incised; c-j. St. Clair Plain; k-t. Crable Trailed; u-v. Wells Incised; w-y. Crable Trailed; z-f'. Crable Deep Rimmed Plate.

PLATE VII

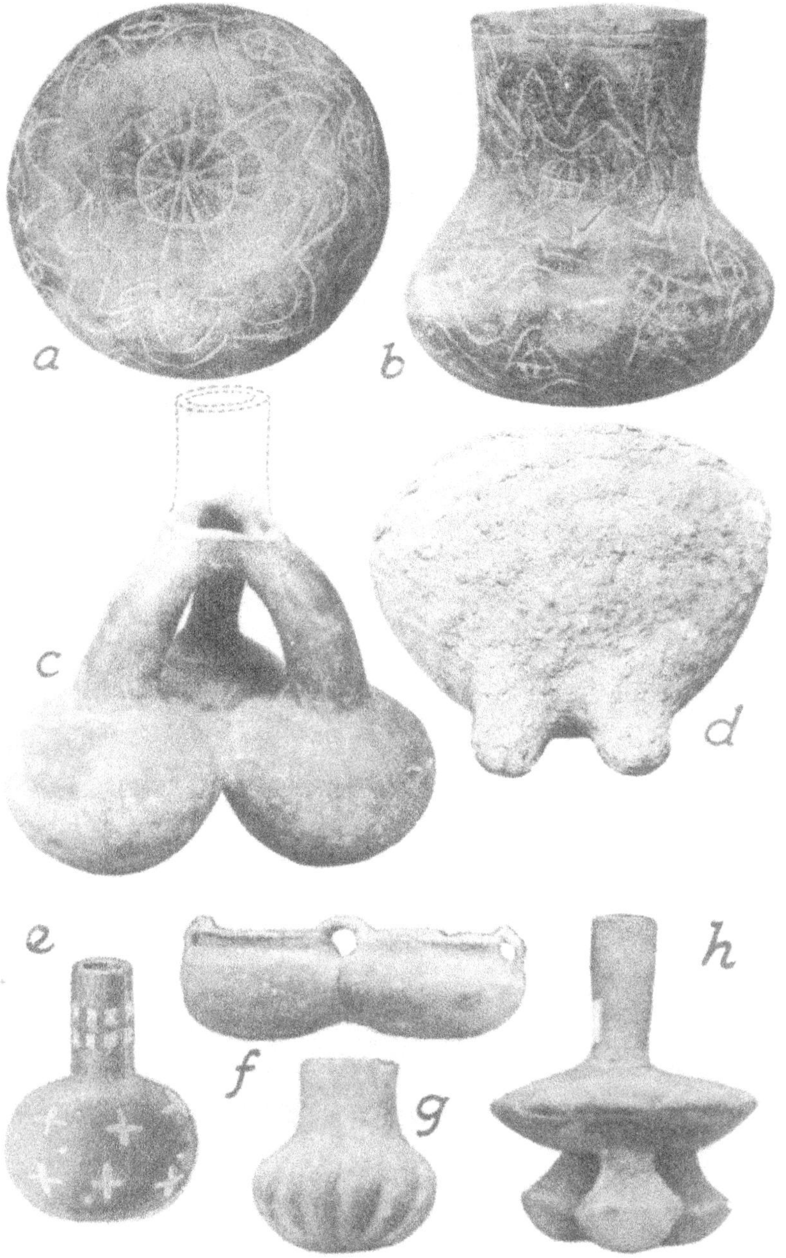

ɔ. Kerton Incised vessels; c. Old Town Red water bottle; d. Prob-
matical conical vessel; e. Negative painted water bottle; f. Crable
ain horizontal compound vessel; g. St. Clair Plain water bottle;
Bell Plain water bottle.

PLATE VIII

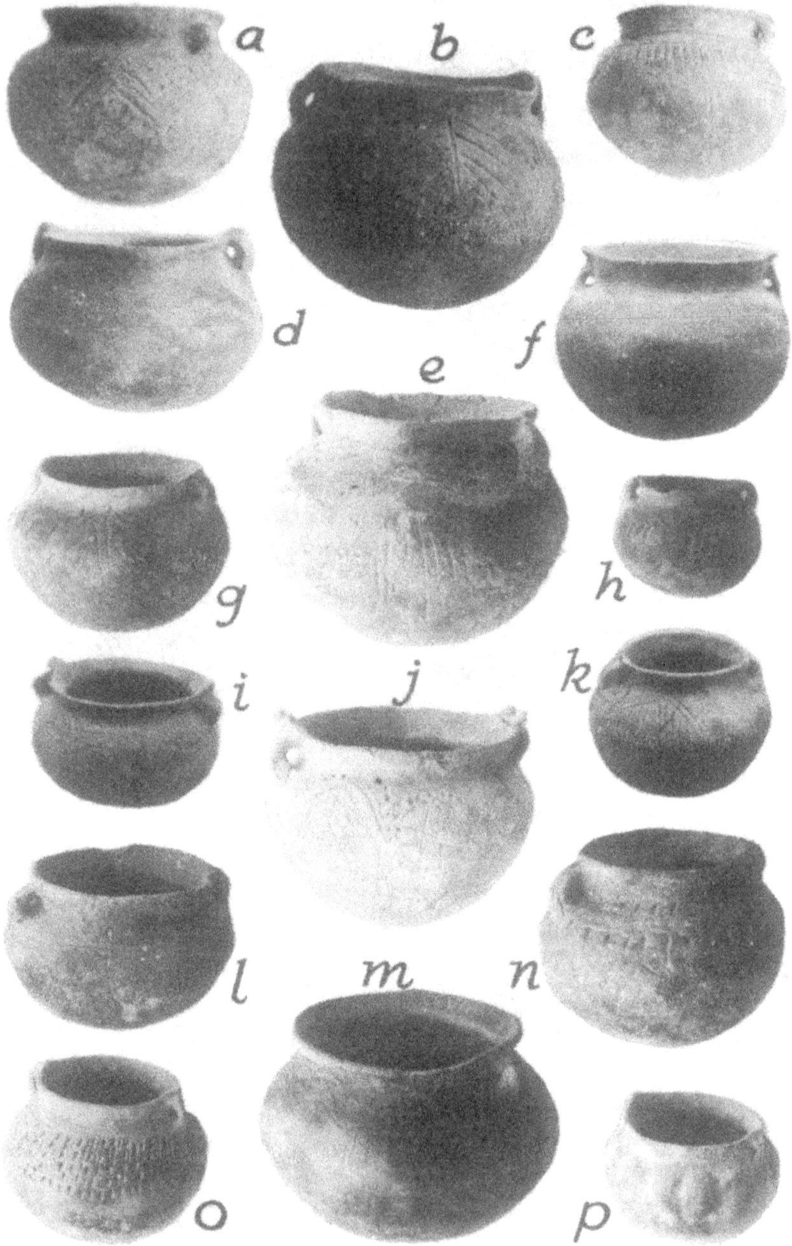

a-c. Crable Trailed; d. Crable Plain; e. Crable Trailed; f. Crabl Cord-Marked; g-h. Crable Trailed; i. Crable Plain; j-p. Crable Trailed.

PLATE IX

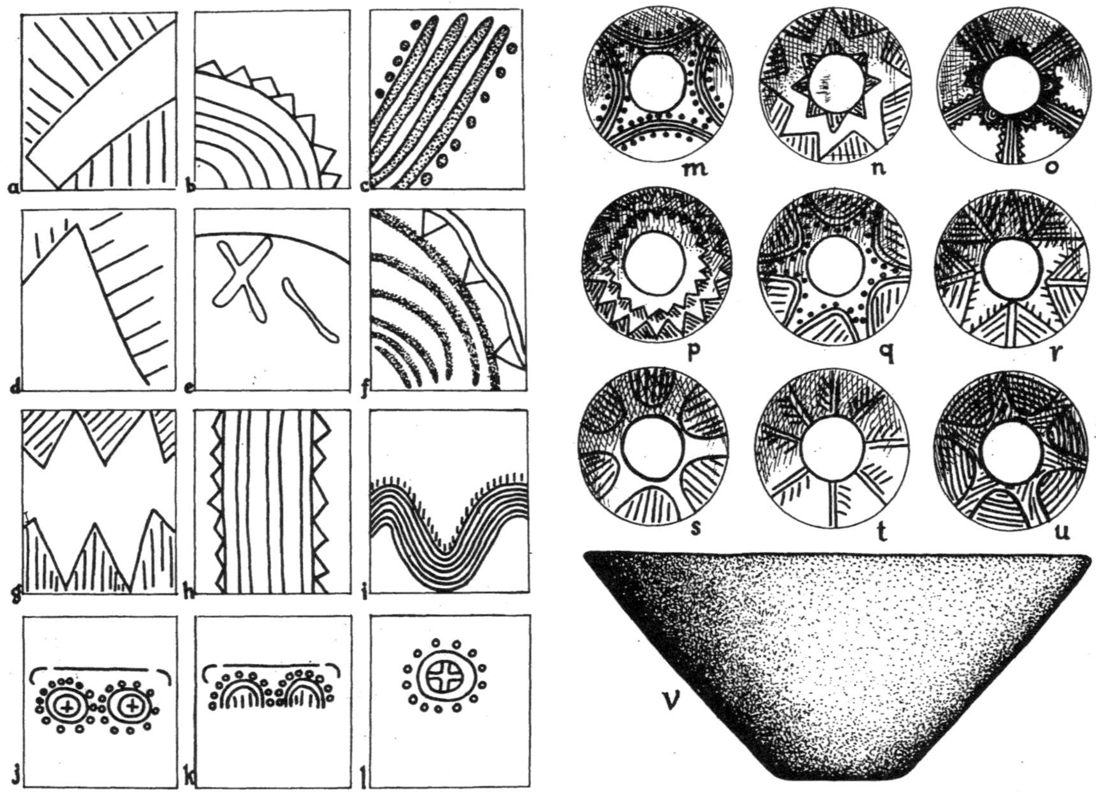

a-i. Wells Incised motifs; j-l. Crable Trailed jar decoration; m-u. Crable Deep Rimmed Plate motifs; v. Side view of Crable Deep Rimmed Plate.

PLATE X

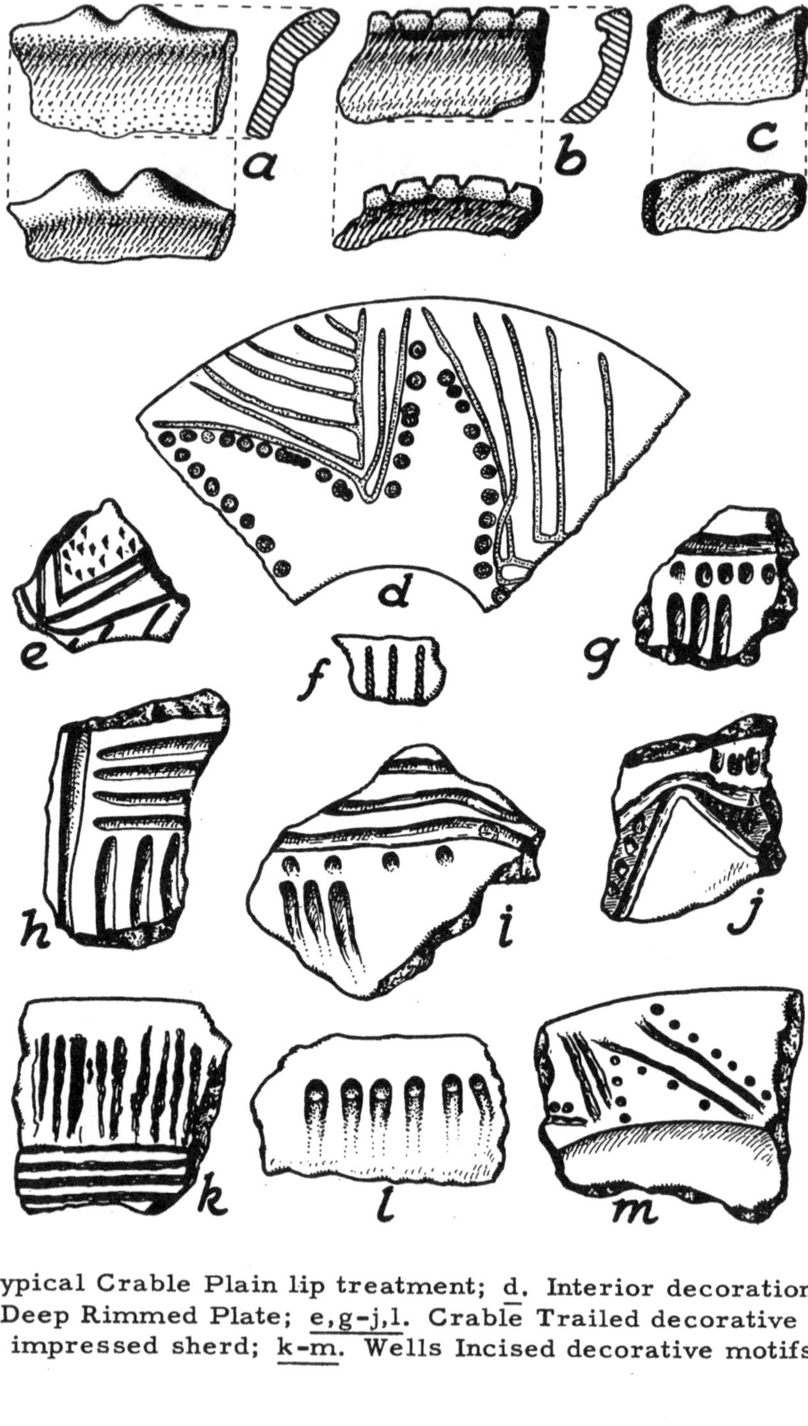

a-c. Atypical Crable Plain lip treatment; d. Interior decoration of Crable Deep Rimmed Plate; e,g-j,l. Crable Trailed decorative moti f. Cord impressed sherd; k-m. Wells Incised decorative motifs.

PLATE XI

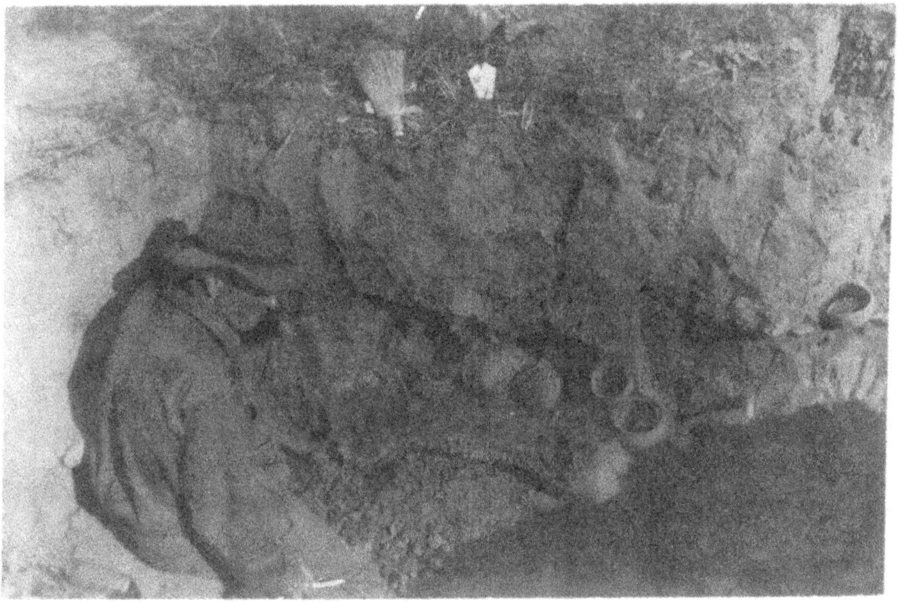

a. McGirr and excavation in Fc896.

b. Two Crable Cord-Marked sherds.

PLATE XII

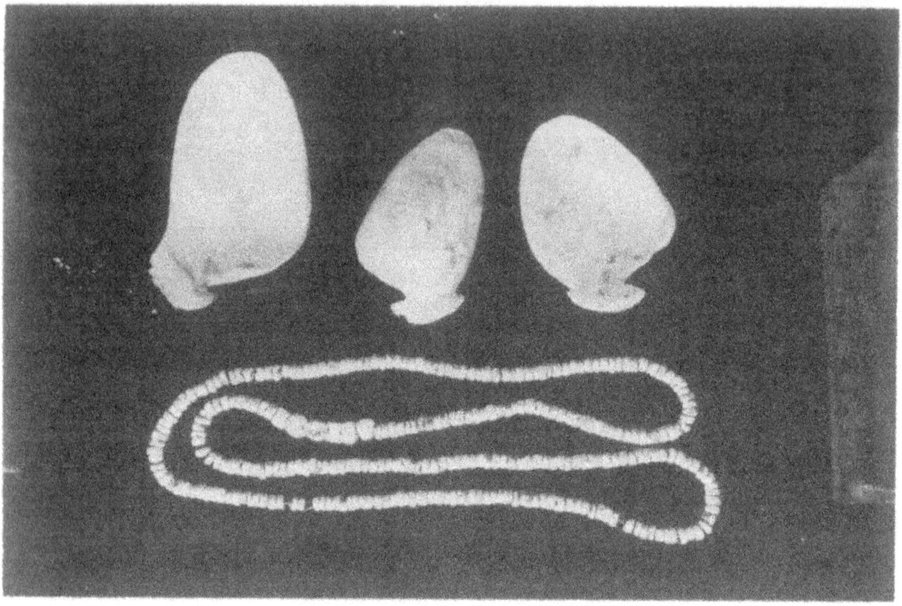

Artifacts: a. Shell spoons and beads.

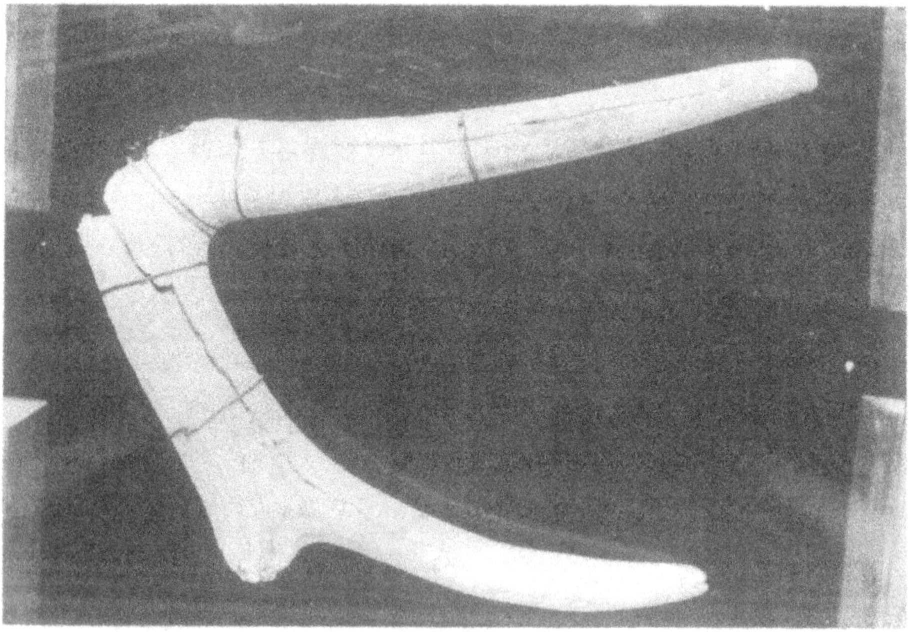

b. Elk antler hoe.

www.ingramcontent.com/pod-product-compliance
Lightning Source LLC
LaVergne TN
LVHW050022250826
846302LV00008B/64